FLAVOURS OF

Aleppo

English edition published by Whitecap Books, 2013

Whitecap Books is known for its expertise in the cookbook market, and has produced some of the most innovative and familiar titles found in kitchens across North America. Visit our website at www.whitecap.ca.

EDITOR | Theresa Best
DESIGNER | Michelle Furbacher
TRANSLATOR | Marcella Walton
FOOD PHOTOGRAPHY | Tango
ALEPPO PHOTOGRAPHY | Ivan Vdovin / Getty Images (page iii, 107), DEA / C. SAPPA / Getty Images (page iv, 6, 7), Christian Kober / Alamy (page iv, 38), Holger Leue / Getty Images (page v, 60), jackmalipan / iStockphoto.com (page v, 106), Donata Pizzi / Getty Images (page v, 120), Bruno Morandi / Getty Images (page x), EmmePi Images / Alamy (page 2), Tim Barker / Getty Images (page 24 [top], 39, 157), Hemis / Alamy (page 24 [bottom]), pacaypalla / iStockphoto.com (page 47), tunart / iStockphoto.com (page 61, 121), Jim Grover / Alamy (page 74 [bottom]), ugurhan / iStockphoto.com (page 93 [top left]), Christopher Herwig / Getty Images (page 93 [top right]), Francesco Lorenzetti / Getty Images (page 93 [bottom]), Patrick Syder Images / Getty Images (page 116 [top left and bottom]), Image Courtesy of Jennifer Hayes / Getty Images (page 116 [top right]), falasha / iStockphoto.com (151)

Printed in Canada

LIBRARY AND ARCHIVES CANADA CATALOGUING IN PUBLICATION

Kadé-Badra, Dalal

    Flavours of Aleppo : celebrating Syrian cuisine / Dalal Kadé-Badra and Elie Badra.

Includes index.

Translation of: Saveurs d'Alep.

ISBN 978-1-77050-178-2

1. Cooking--Syria--Aleppo. 2. Cooking, Syrian. 3. Cookbooks. I. Badra, Elie II. Title.

TX725.S9K3213 2013   641.595691'3   C2013-900087-9

The publisher acknowledges the financial support of the Government of Canada through the Canada Book Fund (CBF) and the Province of British Columbia through the Book Publishing Tax Credit.

13 14 15 16 17   5 4 3 2 1

ENVIRONMENTAL BENEFITS STATEMENT

Whitecap Books Ltd saved the following resources by printing the pages of this book on chlorine free paper made with 10% post-consumer waste.

TREES	WATER	ENERGY	SOLID WASTE	GREENHOUSE GASES
8	3,671	3	246	677
FULLY GROWN	GALLONS	MILLION BTUs	POUNDS	POUNDS

Environmental impact estimates were made using the Environmental Paper Network Paper Calculator 3.2. For more information visit www.papercalculator.org.

FLAVOURS OF

Aleppo

Celebrating Syrian Cuisine

· · · · · · · · · · · · · · · · · ·

DALAL KADÉ-BADRA
& ELIE BADRA

whitecap

CONTENTS

....

APPETIZERS AND SALADS

Mazza et Salata

7

VEGETARIAN DISHES

Siyemie

39

CONTENTS

APPETIZERS AND SALADS

Mazza et Salata

7

VEGETARIAN DISHES

Siyemié

39

FLAVOURS OF
Aleppo

Celebrating Syrian Cuisine

· · · · · · · · · · · · · · · · ·

DALAL KADÉ-BADRA
& ELIE BADRA

whitecap

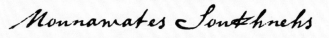

MY MOTHER'S CUISINE

ELIE BADRA WRITES—Of all the many diverse images from my childhood running through my imagination, those connected to familial cuisine are the most memorable. Memories of the aromas wafting from my mother's kitchen are ingrained in me and are what prompted me to write this book with her. My mother inherited her culinary knowledge from her mother, my grandmother, originally from Aleppo, a city with a well-established reputation in gastronomy.

For us, cooking always held the central position, like a vital organ in our home. It was tradition for relatives to come over to take part in feasts, without notice. This never bothered my mother; she always prepared larger amounts of food than necessary for our immediate family.

My mother's cuisine was not only limited to preparation. She gave importance to the table decoration, which seduced the eyes before dishes satisfied the taste buds. I remember her ingenious ideas, substituting the ingredients of Aleppo, often impossible to find in Quebec when I was a child, for available local products that didn't alter traditional flavours.

It is my mother's ingenuity that I wanted to share in this book. You will discover one hundred and one things that make up the delicacies of Aleppian food, the results of a highly refined ancestral cuisine. All this said, I now hand it over to my mother.

DALAL KADÉ-BADRA WRITES—With this book, much like my son Elie, I want to pay tribute to my mother, a wonderful woman, blessed with the patience of an angel, who passed on her passion for cooking. My mother, above all, instilled in me the importance of presentation and plating. From the harmonious mix of ingredients through the worry of cooking until the visual appeal of the final result, everything counts in the preparation of a meal. This is what she taught me. **(CONTINUED ON NEXT PAGE)**

Through these pages, I hope to give credit to my mother's cooking and to have you discover the flavours of Aleppo. Curiously, it is my son Elie, who always wanted to learn the family recipes and was quick to execute them, that gave me the desire to give you mine.

We, the women of Aleppo, for generations, have passed down from mother to daughter a culinary tradition that has never stopped evolving, enriching and refining. As such, it goes without saying that from house to house, there is always a little something, a variation distilling a particular flavour, that differentiates us from each other yet never opposes us.

ACKNOWLEDGEMENTS

I would like to thank my husband for his patience and support, as well as my two sons, Elie and Rémi, who helped me through this project. I would also like to thank Pierre, who pushed and encouraged me for twenty-five years to write a book, and Suzanne, who made this dream a reality. Didier, thank you so much for always being there for me when I needed you. Also, thank you to Simon, Rémi and Dima for their help editing the texts.

I am grateful for the team at Éditions de l'Homme, especially for Pascale Mongeon, Linda Nantel and Erwan Leseul, who backed me during the production of this book.

Finally, a huge thank-you to my family, friends and acquaintances who encouraged me or helped in their own way at one point or another during this creative work. Your names are written on my heart with gratitude.

—Dalal Kadé-Badra

INTRODUCTION

Between the Euphrates and the Mediterranean, on the silk and spice road, Aleppo is one of the most ancient cities of the world. As a crossroad between the East and the West, it has been for thousands of years a strategic and hybrid city. It is the second largest city in Syria and its gastronomical capital.

The food of Aleppo originates from Persian, European, Asian and Ottoman influences. This elaborate culinary art is characterized by two techniques: that of puff pastry, heritage from Persian cuisine, and that of stuffing, of Ottoman heritage, very useful for tripe and hollowed-out vegetables. The creativity and imagination of Aleppian women has transformed a simple mix of meat and bulgur into a very complex art, the kibbeh, which can be cooked in the oven, pan fried, boiled, grilled or eaten raw.

For the inhabitants of Aleppo, food is a domain of sharing and joie de vivre. Plates are prepared in large quantities and are laid out to form a sort of buffet where everyone can serve themselves as they please. Whether there are six, ten or fifty guests, all are welcome and there is always more than enough to enjoy. A meal with invited guests is normally made up of four or five appetizers, two entrées and two desserts. There is something for every palate.

Another typical trait of Aleppian cuisine is a skillful mix of sweet and salty. Fruits or certain desserts are often served with cheese while meat can be accompanied by a cherry or grenadine sauce. In the never-ending quest for innovation, flavours and aromas marry with taste.

Even though Middle Eastern products are more readily available in the West, certain foods are still little known. Included in this book is a glossary of some of the ingredients typical of the cuisine of Aleppo as well as some equipment essential for Aleppian cooking.

(a)

(c)
(b)

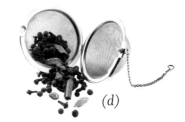
(d)

GLOSSARY OF INGREDIENTS AND EQUIPMENT

ALEPPO CHEESE *(fig. a)*

Aleppo cheese is a simple, mild, unripened, semi-soft cheese made from fresh curd in a saltwater brine. To braid the cheese, melt it in water, stretch it, braid it by hand and put it in brine to conserve it. Braided cheese can be kept for up to a year. Before eating, rinse the cheese in cold water to wash away the excess salt. Cubed cheese is stored in brine and is best when consumed fresh, only a few days old.

ALEPPO CHERRIES (KARAZ AL HALABI)

Similar to Morello cherries, cherries from Aleppo (*al Halabi* means "from Aleppo") are very dark-skinned and acidic. They are used to make jam, sorbet or liqueur.

ALEPPO PEPPER

Aleppo pepper is a fragrant and fruity pepper cultivated in the region of Aleppo. It heightens the flavour of traditional dishes, and is hot but not as spicy as cayenne pepper. Ground Aleppo pepper is found in specialty and Middle Eastern grocery stores.

BULGUR (BOURGHOL) *(fig. b)*

Bulgur is durum wheat that has been shucked from its husk, parboiled, dried and then crushed. It is sold in number 1, 2 and 3 grinds, number 1 being the most fine.

CLARIFIED BUTTER (BUTTER OIL, SAMNEH OR GHEE)

Clarified butter is liquid milk fat that has been rendered from butter. Butter is melted, and the solids and impurities are separated and removed from the butter fat. Clarified butter stores better and withstands higher temperatures than ordinary butter. Clarified butter can be used in place of ordinary butter in any recipe in this book.

(e) (f) (g)

DAKKA *(fig. d)*

Dakka is a mixture of spices ground by the cook or left whole, depending on the recipe. In this book, the mixture used is allspice (40%), ground black pepper (30%), crushed cinnamon (10%), whole cloves (10%), whole green cardamom (5%) and ground nutmeg (5%). The dakka mixture is often put into a spice infuser, which can then be attached to a pot so that the mixture can cook along with the food.

FREEKEH *(fig. e)*

Always present in festive meals, freekeh is young green wheat.

HABRA

Habra is very lean ground meat, either beef or lamb. It is available in Middle Eastern grocery stores.

HANSA

In mid-May, the flowers of the hansa rose invade the city's markets. It is at this time that each family makes their jars of rose-petal jam.

KIBBEH

Kibbeh is a mixture of habra meat, bulgur, onion, fine salt and water, which is then shaped into little balls or other shapes.

LABAN

Laban is traditional Middle Eastern yogurt. It has a sour taste. In grocery stores, it is referred to as Mediterranean-style yogurt.

MECHWI

Mechoui is Middle Eastern grilled meat. Depending on the customs of each country, different types of meat are used, but most often lamb, chicken or beef is used.

MIDDLE EASTERN OMELETTE PAN *(fig. f)*

Middle Eastern omelette pans are aluminum, and similar to blini or crêpe pans. They can usually be found in Middle Eastern grocery stores.

MOLASSES *(fig. g)*

Molasses (which comes in different flavours—pomegranate, grape and raisin, for example)

(h)

(i)

is used in many savoury dishes to give them a slightly acidic taste.

PISTACHIOS *(fig. h)*

Pistachios are small nuts that grow in Aleppo. They should be harvested once they have cracked open (under a full moon at the end of summer!).

POMEGRANATE *(fig. i)*

The pomegranate is a large fruit with edible seeds. The end of August marks the beginning of pomegranate season. Three varieties of pomegranate grow in Aleppo: sweet (*helou*), acidic (*laffan*) and sour (*hamod*). Pomegranate juice is used throughout the year.

SUMAC *(fig. c)*

Sumac is a spice derived from the seed of the *Rhus* plant, a shrub native to Turkey. Its slightly acidic flavour and fragrance heighten the taste of salads. It is found, ground, in Middle Eastern grocery stores. North American sumac is an ornamental shrub, inedible and very toxic.

VERJUICE

Verjuice is an acidic juice made of unripe green grapes. It is found in some Middle Eastern grocery stores. In the recipes in this book, it can be replaced in a pinch by freshly squeezed lemon juice.

Mazza et Salata

APPETIZERS AND SALADS

Yolangi Halabi

STUFFED MINIATURE EGGPLANT

PREPARATION TIME 45 minutes   **COOKING TIME** 30 to 45 minutes   **SERVINGS** 8 to 10

2 Tbsp (30 mL) olive oil

1 onion, minced

½ cup (125 mL) medium-grain rice, rinsed well

½ cup (125 mL) fresh flat-leaf parsley, chopped

¼ cup (60 mL) walnuts, chopped roughly

1 Tbsp (15 mL) pomegranate molasses

½ tsp (2 mL) fine salt

½ tsp (2 mL) ground Aleppo pepper

½ tsp (2 mL) dakka

15 to 18 miniature eggplants

2 Tbsp (30 mL) pomegranate molasses

2 Tbsp (30 mL) fresh lemon juice

1 tsp (5 mL) fine salt

In a large pan, heat the olive oil on high heat. Brown the onions and the rice for 4 to 5 minutes. Add the parsley, walnuts, pomegranate molasses, salt, Aleppo pepper and dakka. Cook on low heat for 5 minutes and set aside.

Cut off the tops of the eggplants. Scoop out and reserve the eggplant flesh for another time. Wash and drain the eggplants. (You may want to salt, allow to stand for 20 minutes, rinse and pat dry the eggplants to prepare them.) Stuff the eggplants with the stuffing without packing too hard (the rice can cause the eggplant to explode during cooking).

Arrange the eggplants in a pot, cut tops facing upwards. Add the pomegranate molasses, lemon juice and salt overtop. Add enough water to reach the top of the eggplants. Place an overturned plate on the eggplants to keep them submerged and in place. Bring to a boil. Reduce the heat to low and leave simmering for 30 to 45 minutes, until a fork can pierce the skin of the eggplant.

Babaghanouj bel Reman

BABAGHANOUJ WITH POMEGRANATE

There are many varieties of eggplant. I use medium-size, purple eggplant. Its flesh is white and spongy and it contains fewer seeds. Also, for this recipe it tastes less bitter. If you're cooking this recipe in winter, or don't want to use the barbeque, grill the eggplant in a 450°F (230°C) oven.

PREPARATION TIME 15 minutes **COOKING TIME** 30 minutes **SERVINGS** 6 to 8

3 medium eggplants

2 cups (500 mL) tomatoes, chopped

1 cup (250 mL) fresh flat-leaf parsley, chopped

1 cup (250 mL) green bell pepper, diced

1 tsp (5 mL) puréed garlic

2 Tbsp (30 mL) fresh lemon juice

1 tsp (5 mL) fine salt

¼ cup (60 mL) olive oil

½ cup (125 mL) pomegranate juice

½ cup (125 mL) pomegranate seeds

Preheat the barbeque. Oil the grill with vegetable oil. Prick the eggplants with a fork and grill on the barbeque for 30 minutes, or until soft, making sure to turn them over every so often.

Quickly peel the eggplants while they are still hot. Place in a large bowl. With an immersion blender, give a few quick pulses to the eggplant flesh.

In another bowl, mix the tomatoes, parsley, bell pepper, garlic, lemon juice, salt, olive oil, pomegranate juice and half of the pomegranate seeds. Mix the tomato and pomegranate mixture with the puréed eggplant. Decorate with the remaining pomegranate seeds.

Ïtche

BULGUR AND POMEGRANATE SALAD

Ïtche is a variation of tabbouleh, and there are dozens of ways to make it.
Here is my family's favourite.

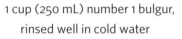

PREPARATION TIME 45 minutes   **COOKING TIME** 30 minutes   **SERVINGS** 6 to 8

1 cup (250 mL) number 1 bulgur, rinsed well in cold water

3 cups (750 mL) tomatoes, diced finely

1½ cups (375 mL) fresh parsley, chopped

1 cup (250 mL) green bell pepper, diced finely

1 cup (250 mL) onion, diced finely

½ tsp (2 mL) salt

VINAIGRETTE

3 Tbsp (45 mL) pomegranate molasses

1 Tbsp (15 mL) tomato paste

1 tsp (5 mL) chili pepper paste

2 tsp (10 mL) salt

1 Tbsp (15 mL) fresh lemon juice

¾ cup (185 mL) olive oil

Put the bulgur into a large salad bowl. Add the tomatoes and let sit, so the bulgur can absorb the juices of the tomatoes, for 30 minutes. Add the parsley, bell pepper, onions and salt. Mix well.

In another bowl, add the pomegranate molasses, tomato paste, chili pepper paste, salt, fresh lemon juice and olive oil and mix well. Pour over the bulgur and tomato salad and mix well.

Mhammara

RED PEPPER AND WALNUT DIP

This dip (pictured on page 19) goes well with Aleppian Mortadella (page 18).

PREPARATION TIME 15 to 30 minutes   **SERVINGS** 10 to 12

8 red bell peppers, chopped roughly

3 small chili peppers, chopped roughly

⅓ cup (80 mL) olive oil

2 tsp (10 mL) fine salt

1 cup (250 mL) breadcrumbs

2 Tbsp (30 mL) pomegranate molasses

2 Tbsp (30 mL) fresh lemon juice

1½ cups (375 mL) walnuts, chopped

whole walnuts, for garnish

Using a food processor, purée the chopped red bell peppers and chili peppers. Add the olive oil and salt and mix to make a smooth paste. Pour into a large bowl. Add the breadcrumbs, pomegranate molasses, lemon juice and chopped nuts. Mix well. Serve in a serving bowl and garnish with some whole walnuts.

Chouti Stambouli

LEMON ARTICHOKE HEARTS AND CARROTS

I love artichokes, whether barbequed, marinated or raw in a good salad. As soon as I see them in the market, I want to buy them. The impulse is stronger than me.

PREPARATION TIME 40 to 60 minutes **COOKING TIME** 30 to 45 minutes **SERVINGS** 8 to 10

10 large artichoke hearts
12 ounces (375 g) baby carrots
20 pearl onions
½ cup (125 mL) peas
1 cup (250 mL) olive oil
2 tsp (10 mL) fine salt
1 tsp (5 mL) ground allspice
½ cup (125 mL) fresh lemon juice
2 cups (500 mL) water

Remove the chokes from the artichoke hearts. (To avoid discolouration, put the artichoke hearts into lemon water until ready to cook. Drain before cooking.) In a large bowl, mix the carrots, onions, peas, olive oil, salt, allspice and lemon juice.

In a large shallow saucepan, place each artichoke heart. Add a spoonful of the vegetable mixture to the bowl of each artichoke heart. Add the water just to the edge of the filled artichoke hearts. Do not cover. Bring to a boil. Reduce the heat and let simmer for 30 to 45 minutes, until the vegetables are cooked, adding more water if necessary. Cool before serving.

Sonjo

SPICY SAUSAGES

These sausages are delicious in a sandwich with sliced tomatoes and pickles (I often grill the sandwich in a panini press). If you don't want to make sandwiches, add two diced tomatoes to the cooked sausages, cook for an extra five minutes and serve.

PREPARATION TIME 30 minutes **COOKING TIME** 10 minutes **SERVINGS** 6 to 8

2 pounds (1 kg) lean ground beef

2 tsp (10 mL) ground cumin

1 Tbsp (15 mL) fine salt

1 Tbsp (15 mL) ground dakka

1 Tbsp (15 mL) puréed garlic

1 Tbsp (15 mL) chili pepper paste

1 Tbsp (15 mL) tomato paste

3 Tbsp (45 mL) butter

In a large bowl, mix the beef with the cumin, salt, dakka, garlic, chili pepper paste and tomato paste. Shape the sausages 1 inch (2.5 cm) in diameter and 5 inches (12 cm) in length. Put on a cookie sheet lined with parchment paper. Cover and freeze for 12 to 24 hours.

When ready to cook the sausages, take them out of the freezer and cut, on the diagonal, into ½-inch (1 cm) pieces. In a large pan, melt and brown the butter on high heat. Cook the sausages for 3 to 4 minutes on each side. (Using frozen sausages ensures they keep their form.) Serve on a ciabatta bun with sliced tomatoes and pickles.

Mortadella Halbye

ALEPPIAN MORTADELLA

This goes well with Red Pepper and Walnut Dip, pictured here (see page 13 for recipe).

PREPARATION TIME 30 to 40 minutes **COOKING TIME** 30 minutes **SERVINGS** 10 to 12

2 pounds (1 kg) habra meat

2 Tbsp (30 mL) puréed garlic

2 Tbsp (30 mL) fine salt

2 Tbsp (30 mL) ground dakka

1 cup (250 mL) pistachios, shelled

fine salt, for seasoning

ground dakka, for seasoning

3 cups (750 mL) red wine vinegar

1½ cups (375 mL) water

1 Tbsp (15 mL) salt

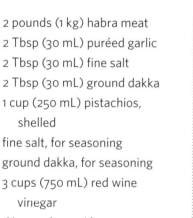

In a large bowl, mix the habra meat with the garlic, salt and dakka. Separate into 3 portions. Wet the bottom of a plate. Spread one portion on the plate, making a circle 8 inches (20 cm) in diameter. Cover uniformly with the pistachios, making sure they stick. Season with salt and dakka. Wet hands with water and tightly roll the meat to form a large roll. Smooth the roll with water, closing the ends carefully and making sure they stick. (See photos.) Repeat with the other two portions of meat.

In a large pot, bring the vinegar, water and salt to a boil. Gently put the rolls into the pot; cover and bring to a boil. Reduce to low heat and simmer for 30 minutes, until the meat is cooked. Remove the rolls and place them on a cookie sheet. Cover well with plastic wrap, place a weighted object overtop and let cool. Refrigerate the rolls in an airtight container. Serve with Red Pepper and Walnut Dip (page 13).

Saltet el Zahra

CAULIFLOWER SALAD

Use white, green and purple cauliflower, if you can find all three varieties. To make this salad even more colourful, add whole cherry tomatoes. This recipe yields a large quantity and keeps for several days in the refrigerator.

PREPARATION 30 minutes   **SERVINGS** 10 to 12

¼ cup (60 mL) apple cider vinegar

2 tsp (10 mL) fine salt

¼ tsp (1 mL) ground black pepper

¼ tsp (1 mL) ground Aleppo pepper

2 Tbsp (30 mL) vegetable seasoning (purchased)

¼ cup (60 mL) olive oil

1 red onion, sliced thinly

2 pounds (1 kg) cauliflower (white, green and purple varieties), cut into small florets

2½ cups (625 mL) broccoli, cut into small florets

1½ cups (375 mL) carrots, sliced thinly

1½ cups (375 mL) celery, sliced thinly

1 cup (250 mL) dried cranberries

1 cup (250 mL) slivered almonds, roasted

In a large salad bowl, mix the cider vinegar, salt, black pepper, Aleppo pepper, vegetable seasoning and olive oil. Add the onion slices and mix well. Add the cauliflower, broccoli, carrots, celery, cranberries and almonds. Toss well.

Kibbeh bel Baid

EGG IN KIBBEH

This dish can be very prettily presented. You can complement the red of the pomegranate-seed garnish with diced red, green and yellow bell peppers as well as fresh mint and parsley. The various colours of the dish are why my mother always liked to include it in a selection of appetizers.

PREPARATION TIME 60 minutes **COOKING TIME** 20 minutes **SERVINGS** 10 to 12

8 large eggs
1 small onion, grated
1 cup (250 mL) number 1 bulgur
1 tsp (5 mL) fine salt
¾ to 1 cup (185 to 250 mL) water
8 ounces (250 g) habra meat
pomegranate seeds, for garnish

Put the eggs in a large pot and cover them with water. Salt the water, bring to a boil and cook for 8 to 10 minutes, until the eggs are hardboiled. Rinse the cooked eggs under cold water, and dry and shell them. Set aside. In a large bowl, mix the onion, bulgur and salt. Add the water and mix. Gradually add the meat and keep mixing until the dough becomes easy to work with. (Wet your hands with cold water to prevent the dough from becoming too sticky.) Divide the dough into 8 portions and shape into balls. Place a ball in the palm of your hand. (See photos page 73.) Stick the index finger of your other hand into the ball to make a hole from one end to the other without piercing it. Create a well and press lightly. Pivot the kibbeh until it forms an eggcup shape. Put an egg in the cavity and close the opening.

Bring a large pot of salted water to a boil. Add the egg in kibbeh and cook on high heat for 10 minutes, until the meat is cooked. Remove the egg in kibbeh from the water, let cool and refrigerate in an airtight container. Cut each egg in kibbeh in 4 lengthwise. Arrange on a platter. Garnish with pomegranate seeds.

Djedj Tarator

TAHINI CHICKEN

You can replace the chicken with the same quantity of cubed Angus beef strip loin. I recommend that you prepare puréed garlic in a large quantity with the help of a food processor. Add olive oil to help with the chopping. The puréed garlic will keep for a month in the refrigerator in an airtight jar, and you will always have the necessary amount within reach. This dish is especially attractive when garnished with black olives, parsley and red peppers.

PREPARATION TIME 15 minutes   **COOKING TIME** 45 minutes   **SERVINGS** 6 to 8

1 pound (500 g) skinless, boneless chicken breast
1 Tbsp (15 mL) dakka, whole in a spice infuser
1 small onion, quartered
1 tsp (5 mL) fine salt
1 cup (250 mL) tahini (sesame seed paste)
¼ cup (60 mL) fresh lemon juice
1 tsp (5 mL) puréed garlic
1 tsp (5 mL) fine salt
1 cup (250 mL) water
3 Tbsp (45 mL) yogurt

Put the chicken in a large pot, cover with water and bring to a boil. Skim the fat from the surface, attach the spice infuser to the pot and add the onions and salt. Let simmer on low heat for 30 to 45 minutes, until the chicken is cooked through. Remove the chicken from the pot and let it cool. Shred the meat using a fork and set aside.

Mix the tahini, lemon juice, garlic, salt, water and yogurt. Reserve ½ cup (125 mL) of the tahini mixture. Gradually add the remaining tahini mixture to the meat and mix. Place the chicken on a serving platter and add the reserved tahini sauce overtop.

Salijo

ALEPPO SAUSAGES

Aleppo Sausages and Spicy Sausages (page 17) are traditionally made in a casing. I've adapted the recipes so that the preparation is less time consuming and complicated. These go well with Potato Salad (facing page).

PREPARATION TIME 30 minutes **COOKING TIME** 10 to 15 minutes **SERVINGS** 6 to 8

2 pounds (1 kg) lean ground beef
1 Tbsp (15 mL) fine salt
1½ Tbsp (22 mL) ground dakka
¼ cup (60 mL) pine nuts
3 Tbsp (45 mL) butter

In a large bowl, mix the beef, salt, dakka and pine nuts. Make sausages 1½ inches (4 cm) in length. In a large pan melt and brown the butter on high heat. Sear the sausages for two minutes on each side.

Banadora ma Bassal

TOMATO AND ONION SALAD

This salad goes well with pita bread.

PREPARATION TIME 15 minutes **SERVINGS** 4 to 6

2 cups (500 mL) tomatoes, cubed
½ onion, diced
3 Tbsp (45 mL) olive oil
½ tsp (2 mL) fine salt
¼ tsp (1 mL) ground Aleppo pepper

In a salad bowl, mix the tomatoes and onion. In another bowl, mix the olive oil, salt and Aleppo pepper. Pour the oil mixture over the vegetables and toss well.

Saltet el Batateh

POTATO SALAD

I often prepare this salad at the last minute because the flavours are more pronounced when the potatoes are still warm. It keeps for two to three days in the refrigerator.

PREPARATION TIME 15 minutes **COOKING TIME** 30 to 45 minutes **SERVINGS** 4 to 6

2 pounds (1 kg) whole potatoes, unpeeled
¼ cup (60 mL) fresh lemon juice
1 tsp (5 mL) fine salt
1 tsp (5 mL) ground allspice
¼ cup (60 mL) olive oil
½ cup (125 mL) onions, diced
½ cup (125 mL) fresh parsley, chopped

Cook the potatoes in a pot of salted boiling water for about 30 minutes, or until tender.

In a bowl, mix the lemon juice, salt, allspice and olive oil. Add the onions and parsley and mix. Set aside.

Rinse the potatoes in cold water. Peel immediately and cut into ¾-inch (2 cm) cubes. Put the potatoes in a salad bowl. Pour the vinaigrette overtop and toss well.

Saltet el Chamandar

BEET SALAD

PREPARATION TIME 30 minutes   **SERVINGS** 4 to 6

3 to 4 medium beets, cooked, peeled and cut into ¾-inch (2 cm) cubes

⅓ cup (80 mL) onions, diced

½ cup (125 mL) fresh parsley, chopped roughly

½ cup (125 mL) pitted green olives

3 Tbsp (45 mL) red wine vinegar

¼ cup (60 mL) olive oil

½ tsp (2 mL) fine salt

In a salad bowl, mix the beets, onions, parsley and olives. Set aside.

In another bowl, mix the vinegar, olive oil and salt. Pour the vinaigrette over the salad and toss well.

Saltet el Laghana

CABBAGE SALAD

This recipe can be made the night before.

PREPARATION TIME 20 minutes   **SERVINGS** 4 to 6

1 medium white cabbage, shredded (4 cups/1 L)
1½ Tbsp (22 mL) red wine vinegar
1 tsp (5 mL) fine salt
½ tsp (2 mL) ground Aleppo pepper
1 tsp (5 mL) dried mint
½ tsp (2 mL) puréed garlic
1 Tbsp (15 mL) fresh lemon juice
½ tsp (2 mL) ground cumin
¼ cup (60 mL) olive oil

Put the cabbage into a large salad bowl. In another bowl, mix the vinegar, salt, Aleppo pepper, mint, garlic, lemon juice, cumin and olive oil. Pour the vinegar mixture over the cabbage and toss well.

Djedj Chartass

RED BELL PEPPER CHICKEN

This recipe is my mother's specialty. She is often asked to make it, and now I'm happy to share it with others.

PREPARATION TIME 20 minutes   **COOKING TIME** 30 to 45 minutes   **SERVINGS** 4 to 6

1 pound (500 g) skinless, boneless chicken breasts

3 cups (750 mL) cold water

1 Tbsp (15 mL) dakka, whole in a spice infuser

3 cups (750 mL) red bell peppers, chopped finely

1 cup (250 mL) walnuts, chopped finely

2 tsp (10 mL) fine salt

¼ tsp (1 mL) ground black pepper

Bring a large pot of water to the boil. Add the chicken breasts and simmer until the chicken is cooked through. Let cool. Skim the fat from the surface of the water and attach the spice infuser to the pot. Lower the heat and let simmer for 30 to 45 minutes, until the chicken breasts are completely cooked. Remove the pot from the heat and let the chicken and broth cool.

In a bowl, mix the chopped bell peppers and walnuts together. Reserve 1 cup (250 mL) of this mixture. Remove the chicken breasts from the broth, reserving the liquid. Shred the breasts.

In a bowl, add the shredded chicken breasts and season with the salt and black pepper. Add 3 cups (750 mL) of the bell pepper and walnut mixture as well as 5 Tbsp (75 mL) of the reserved broth. Mix well. Turn out onto a serving dish. Garnish with the remaining bell pepper and walnut mixture.

Kibbeh Nayeh

KIBBEH TARTAR

This kibbeh, based on uncooked lamb or beef, is typical of the gastronomy of
Aleppo. Usually the onion mixture is kneaded by hand, but you could also use
a food processor. Serve with olive oil and chili pepper paste.

PREPARATION TIME 10 minutes **SERVINGS** 4 to 6

1 onion, grated
¾ cup (185 mL) number 1 bulgur,
    rinsed well in cold water
1 tsp (5 mL) fine salt
¾ to 1 cup (185 to 250 mL) water
1 pound (500 g) habra meat
onion slices
fresh mint leaves

Mix the onion, bulgur, salt and a bit of the water. Knead
the mixture until it becomes sticky. Add the meat and
continue kneading, adding more water a little at a time.
Lay the kibbeh tartar out on a serving plate, shaping it
attractively. Garnish with onion slices and mint leaves.

QUICKLY MADE FALAFELS

In Aleppo, my father never entered the kitchen because it was my mother's domain. When we came to live in Quebec, he was in poor health and the days seemed too long, at times. One day, he wanted to help me in the kitchen and we made falafels. What joy and laughter we shared that day! I will never forget that moment. (Falafel mix—ground chickpeas and spices—is usually sold, boxed, in most supermarkets.)

PREPARATION TIME 15 minutes **COOKING TIME** 20 minutes **YIELD** 12 to 15 patties

BATTER

1 cup (250 mL) falafel mix
   (purchased)
1 tsp (5 mL) baking powder
1 tsp (5 mL) ground cumin
1 tsp (5 mL) ground coriander
¾ cup (175 mL) water
1 egg, beaten
vegetable oil for frying

SAUCE

½ cup (125 mL) tahini (sesame
   seed paste)
2 Tbsp (30 mL) fresh lemon juice
½ tsp (2 mL) fine salt
1½ Tbsp (22 mL) yogurt
½ to ¾ cup (125 to 175 mL) water

BATTER | In a large bowl, mix the falafel mix, baking powder, cumin and coriander with a fork. Add the water and egg. Mix well and let sit for 30 minutes. Heat 1¼ inches (3 cm) vegetable oil in a large pan. Form small patties with the help of a falafel press or by hand. Make a hole in the centre of each patty with your index finger. Fry the patties for 1 to 2 minutes on each side in the hot oil until they become crispy. Set aside.

SAUCE | In a bowl, mix the tahini, lemon juice, salt and yogurt together, gradually adding the water to obtain the desired consistency. Set aside.

To serve, arrange the falafels on a platter with a bowl of diced tomatoes, a bowl of diced pickled turnips and a bowl of the tahini sauce.

To make sandwiches, crush two falafels in a small pita and fill to your liking with the accompaniments.

Saltet Georges
GEORGES' SALAD

This salad is particularly flavourful in the month of August when it is time to harvest sun-ripened tomatoes. My husband, Georges, is crazy about tomatoes, especially when I take the time to skin them. It's a little touch of care that he appreciates. Sometimes, I add two or three tablespoons of pomegranate juice to this recipe.

PREPARATION TIME 10 minutes   **SERVINGS** 4 to 6

2 cups (500 mL) tomatoes, diced
½ cup (125 mL) cucumbers, diced
½ cup (125 mL) green bell peppers, diced
½ cup (125 mL) onions, diced
½ cup (125 mL) fresh parsley, chopped

VINAIGRETTE
¼ cup (60 mL) olive oil
¼ cup (60 mL) fresh lemon juice
¼ tsp (1 mL) ground allspice
1 tsp (5 mL) fine salt

In a salad bowl, mix the tomatoes, cucumbers, bell peppers, onions and parsley. Set aside.

In a small bowl, mix the olive oil, lemon juice, allspice and salt. Pour the vinaigrette over the salad and toss well.

Siyemie

VEGETARIAN DISHES

Makhlouta

LENTIL AND CUMIN SOUP

PREPARATION TIME 10 minutes   **COOKING TIME** 45 to 60 minutes   **SERVINGS** 4 to 6

1 cup (250 mL) red lentils

½ cup (125 mL) long-grain rice,
     rinsed well

¼ cup (60 mL) number 3 bulgur

1 red bell pepper, chopped
     roughly

1 medium onion, grated

2 tsp (10 mL) fine salt

8 cups (2 L) water

2 tsp (10 mL) ground cumin

1 large or 2 small pitas

2 Tbsp (30 mL) olive oil

1 onion, diced

¼ cup (60 mL) olive oil

In a large pot on high heat, bring the lentils, rice, bulgur, bell pepper, onions, salt and water to a boil. Let simmer on medium heat for 45 to 60 minutes, until the lentils and rice are cooked. Stir every so often. Turn off the heat, add the cumin and mix.

Preheat the oven to 350°F (175°C). With scissors, cut the pita into 1-inch (2.5 cm) squares. Brush with the 2 Tbsp (30 mL) of olive oil and cook in the oven for 5 to 10 minutes, until the pita is golden-coloured.

In a pan on high heat, sauté the onions in the ¼ cup (60 mL) olive oil for about 1 minute, until they are translucent. Put the cooked onions and cooking oil into the soup. Mix well and serve. Tableside, add a few pieces of baked pita in each bowl.

Kibbeh Hileh

CRAFTY KIBBEH

Here is a vegetarian version of the famous kibbeh. This recipe can be used in Stuffed Crafty Kibbeh (page 44).

PREPARATION TIME 20 to 30 minutes   **COOKING TIME** 15 minutes   **SERVINGS** 10 to 12

DOUGH

2½ cups (625 mL) number 1 bulgur, rinsed well in cold water
2½ cups (625 mL) all-purpose flour
2 tsp (10 mL) puréed garlic
1 onion, grated
1 Tbsp (15 mL) ground coriander
1 tsp (5 mL) salt
1½ cups (375 mL) water

SAUCE

¼ cup (60 mL) olive oil
2 onions, sliced thinly
1 cup (250 mL) water
6 Tbsp (90 mL) tomato paste
½ cup (125 mL) fresh lemon juice
2 tsp (10 mL) fine salt
flat-leaf parsley, for garnish

DOUGH | Mix the bulgur and flour in a large bowl. Add the garlic, grated onions, coriander and salt. Mix well. Add water, mixing until the batter is malleable. Make little balls about the size of cherries. Boil salted water in a large pot. Cook the kibbeh balls for 5 to 7 minutes, or until the bulgur is cooked. Drain well and set aside.

SAUCE | On high heat in a large pan, brown the sliced onions in the olive oil for 1 minute. Add water, tomato paste, lemon juice and salt. Cook on low heat for 5 to 10 minutes. Place the kibbeh balls into the sauce.

To serve, arrange the Crafty Kibbeh on a platter. Garnish with flat-leaf parsley.

Kibbeh Arbain Chahid

STUFFED CRAFTY KIBBEH

PREPARATION TIME 45 to 60 minutes **COOKING TIME** 20 minutes **YIELD** 65 to 70 balls

STUFFING

3 Tbsp (45 mL) olive oil

2 onions, diced

2 cups (500 mL) fresh parsley, chopped

1 cup (250 mL) walnuts, chopped roughly

1 Tbsp (15 mL) pomegranate molasses

1 tsp (5 mL) fine salt

½ tsp (2 mL) ground Aleppo pepper

1 recipe Crafty Kibbeh dough (page 42)

SAUCE

¼ cup (60 mL) olive oil

2 onions, sliced

½ tsp (2 mL) puréed garlic

6 Tbsp (90 mL) tomato paste

2 Tbsp (30 mL) chili pepper paste

½ cup (125 mL) fresh lemon juice

2 tsp (10 mL) fine salt

1 cup (250 mL) water

STUFFING | In a pan on high heat, brown the onions in the olive oil. Add the parsley, walnuts, pomegranate molasses, salt and Aleppo pepper. Cook for 2 to 3 minutes. Remove from heat and cool. Make the balls with the Crafty Kibbeh dough about the size of prunes. Place a ball in the palm of your hand. Stick the index finger of your other hand into the ball to make a hole from one end to the other without piercing it. Create a well and press lightly. Pivot the kibbeh until it forms an eggcup shape. Stuff with the walnut mixture and close the top carefully. (See page 73 for photographs of this process.) Repeat with all the Kibbeh balls.

SAUCE | In a pot, brown the sliced onions in the olive oil for 1 minute. Add the garlic, tomato paste, chili pepper paste, lemon juice, salt and water. Cook on low heat for 5 to 10 minutes.

Boil salted water in a large pot. Cook the stuffed kibbeh balls for 5 to 7 minutes, or until the bulgur is cooked. Drain well, put in the sauce and serve.

Moujadara

BULGUR AND LENTILS

Everyone wants to eat Moujadara leftovers! One day my mother promised my husband, Georges, she would keep leftovers for him the next day. But surprise! It was my brother who devoured it all early in the morning after spending a long night driving. This dish is delicious with Georges' Salad (page 37).

PREPARATION TIME 10 minutes **COOKING TIME** 20 to 30 minutes **SERVINGS** 4 to 6

2 cups (500 mL) green lentils, rinsed well

4½ cups (1.12 L) water

2 tsp (10 mL) fine salt

1 cup (250 mL) number 2 bulgur

½ cup (125 mL) olive oil

1 large onion, minced

In a large pot, bring to a boil on high heat the lentils, water and salt. Lower the heat to medium and cook for 5 minutes. Add the bulgur and cook for about 10 minutes, until the water has evaporated. Set aside.

In a large pan on high heat, brown the onions in the olive oil until they are caramelized. Remove the onions from the oil and set aside. Pour the cooking oil over the lentils and mix well. Pour onto a serving dish and garnish with the caramelized onions.

Edjet el Chométi

ARTICHOKE OMELETTE

PREPARATION TIME 5 minutes   **COOKING TIME** 5 minutes   **SERVINGS** 4 to 6

6 eggs

4 fresh artichoke hearts, diced finely

1 tsp (5 mL) fine salt

1 tsp (5 mL) ground allspice

1 tsp (5 mL) all-purpose flour

canola oil for cooking

Beat the eggs in a bowl. Add the artichokes, salt, allspice and flour and mix well. In a Middle Eastern omelette pan or a blini pan (see page 4), heat the canola oil on high heat. Add 2 Tbsp (30 mL) of the egg mixture to each divot. Cook on high heat for 1 to 2 minutes on each side, until the omelettes are golden brown. Remove from heat and let rest on a paper towel.

Edjet el Koussa

ZUCCHINI OMELETTE

PREPARATION TIME 5 minutes   **COOKING TIME** 5 minutes   **SERVINGS** 4 to 6

5 eggs

2½ cups (625 mL) zucchini, diced

1 tsp (5 mL) salt

2 tsp (10 mL) ground allspice

2 tsp (10 mL) flour

2 Tbsp (30 mL) pine nuts

canola oil for cooking

Beat the eggs in a bowl. Add the zucchini, salt, allspice, flour and pine nuts. Mix well. In a Middle Eastern omelette pan or a blini pan (see page 4), heat the canola oil on high heat. Add 2 Tbsp (30 mL) of the egg mixture to each divot. Cook on high heat for 1 to 2 minutes on each side, until the omelettes are golden brown. Remove from the heat and let rest on a paper towel. Serve.

Mfarrakeh

SQUASH OMELETTE

When we went to Jean-Talon Market with my mother, Lino from the store called Birri would always put aside small and large squashes for us. You can use either winter or summer squash in this recipe, but I recommend tromboncino squash (a summer vining squash). Use a brush on the squash under cold water to wash well before dicing. Don't use the squash seeds—use only the firm part of the squash.

PREPARATION TIME 20 minutes   **COOKING TIME** 10 minutes   **SERVINGS** 4 to 6

4 cups (1 L) squash, diced very finely
¼ cup (60 mL) butter
8 eggs, beaten
½ tsp (2 mL) fine salt
¾ tsp (4 mL) ground allspice

Spread the diced squash on a microwavable plate. Put in the microwave on maximum power for 2 minutes to dry out the squash. (You can also dry out the squash in an oven.)

In a pan on high heat, cook the dried squash in the butter for 4 to 5 minutes. Add the eggs, salt and allspice. Mix with a wooden spoon (this dish is more like scrambled eggs than a classic omelette). Reduce the heat and cook until the eggs are firm.

Edjet el Batateh

POTATO OMELETTE

PREPARATION TIME 15 minutes   **COOKING TIME** 10 minutes   **SERVINGS** 4 to 6

2 cups (500 mL) mashed
   potatoes
3 eggs, beaten
1 tsp (5 mL) fine salt
1 tsp (5 mL) ground allspice
¼ cup (60 mL) pine nuts
canola oil for cooking

In a bowl, add the potatoes, eggs, salt, allspice and pine nuts and mix well. Set aside. In a Middle Eastern omelette pan or a blini pan (see page 4), heat the canola oil on high heat. Add 2 Tbsp (30 mL) of the potato and egg mixture to each divot. Cook on high heat for 1 to 2 minutes on each side, until the omelettes are dark in colour. Remove from the heat and let rest on a paper towel.

(Alternatively, you can bake the omelette: Preheat the oven to 350°F (175°C) and grease an ovenproof glass dish. Spread a 1-inch (2.5 cm) thick layer of the omelette mixture in the dish and cook 12 to 15 minutes, until the omelette is golden-coloured.)

Edjet el Batdonness

PARSLEY OMELETTE

This is a classic dish for Good Friday. Serve with Aleppo Spread.

PREPARATION TIME 30 minutes   **COOKING TIME** 15 minutes   **SERVINGS** 4 to 6

OMELETTE

7 eggs

1 Tbsp (15 mL) dried mint

1 tsp (5 mL) fine salt

2 tsp (10 mL) ground allspice

1 tsp (5 mL) all-purpose flour

2 cups (500 mL) fresh flat-leaf
parsley, chopped finely

½ onion, grated

1 tsp (5 mL) garlic, chopped
finely

canola oil for cooking

ALEPPO SPREAD

3 cups (750 mL) yogurt

½ cup (125 mL) fresh flat-leaf
parsley, chopped finely

2 Tbsp (30 mL) dried mint, or
½ cup (125 mL) fresh mint,
chopped finely

1 cup (250 mL) romaine lettuce
(the crunchy part in the
middle of the leaf), chopped
very finely

1 tsp (5 mL) garlic, chopped
finely

1 tsp (5 mL) fine salt

OMELETTE | Beat the eggs in a bowl with a fork. Add the mint, salt, allspice and flour. Mix well. Add the parsley, onions and garlic. Mix well. In a Middle Eastern omelette pan or a blini pan (see page 4), heat the canola oil on high heat. Add 2 Tbsp (30 mL) of the egg mixture to each divot. Cook on high heat for 1 to 2 minutes on each side, until the omelettes are dark in colour. Remove from the heat and let rest on a paper towel.

ALEPPO SPREAD | In a bowl, add all the ingredients and mix well.

MOGHRABIEH COUSCOUS

Originally, our grandmothers made couscous by hand. First, they would sprinkle number 3 bulgur with a bit of water, leaving it to swell for 15 minutes. Afterwards, they would roll the grains in flour. Thankfully, today we can buy couscous in stores. To help the onions hold together well during cooking, be sure not to cut off the root ends. This goes well with marinated turnips.

PREPARATION TIME 30 minutes　**COOKING TIME** 15 minutes　**SERVINGS** 4 to 6

25 small pearl onions, peeled but
　roots intact
3 cups (750 mL) water
1 cup (250 mL) couscous
½ cup (125 mL) butter
3 cups (750 mL) chickpeas
1 tsp (5 mL) fine salt

In a large pot, bring the onions and water to a boil. Cook for 5 to 6 minutes. Take the onions out of the pot and set aside, reserving the cooking water. Add the couscous to the cooking water. Cook for 2 to 3 minutes. Drain and set aside.

In a large pot on medium heat, melt the butter. Add the cooked couscous, the cooked onions and the chickpeas and cook until browned. Add the salt and mix for 2 to 3 minutes to coat well.

Chomsi Brombeh

BATTERED ARTICHOKES

You can substitute other vegetables (potato, cauliflower, carrot, zucchini and so on) for the artichokes in this recipe.

MARINATING TIME 2 hours   **COOKING TIME** 10 minutes   **SERVINGS** 4 to 6

5 artichokes, cleaned and cut into ½-inch (1 cm) slices
½ cup (125 mL) olive oil
1 tsp (5 mL) fine salt
½ tsp (2 mL) ground allspice
1 cup (250 mL) all-purpose flour
1½ cups (375 mL) water
1 tsp (5 mL) fine salt
1 tsp (5 mL) ground allspice
canola oil for cooking

In a large bowl, marinate the artichoke slices for 2 hours with the olive oil, salt and allspice.

In another bowl, dilute the flour with water, salt and allspice. Set aside.

Heat the canola oil in a fryer or a large pot. Remove the artichoke slices from the marinade. Place the slices, one at a time, into the batter, taking care to cover them well. Fry in the canola oil a few slices at a time until crispy and golden-coloured.

Rechtayeh

LENTIL AND NOODLE SOUP

PREPARATION TIME 10 minutes   **COOKING TIME** 45 to 50 minutes   **SERVINGS** 4 to 6

2 cups (500 mL) green lentils

2 tsp (10 mL) fine salt

8 cups (2 l) water

¾ cup (185 mL) egg noodles

1 Tbsp (15 mL) all-purpose flour

¼ cup (60 mL) water

2 Tbsp (30 mL) dried mint

1 onion, diced

¼ cup (60 mL) olive oil

In a large pot on medium heat, add the lentils and salt and the 8 cups (2 L) water. Cook for 30 minutes. Add the egg noodles and cook on low heat for 10 to 12 minutes. Dilute the flour in the ¼ cup (60 mL) water and pour into the pot. Mix well and cook for 5 minutes. Turn off the heat. Add the dried mint and cover.

In a very hot pan, sauté the onion in the olive oil on high heat until transparent. Add the sautéed onions to the soup, mix and serve.

Kibbeh Zenglyeh

SPINACH AND CHICKPEA KIBBEH

Instead of throwing out leftover spinach, my mom invited 20 people over to eat Kibbeh Zenglyeh. But this wasn't all—she ended up preparing several other dishes to accompany it. My dad still remarks that it would have been easier to throw out the spinach.

PREPARATION TIME 30 to 45 minutes **COOKING TIME** 10 minutes **YIELD** 12 to 14 pancakes

10 ounces (300 g) spinach, washed, and chopped roughly
1 tsp (5 mL) fine salt
½ cup (125 mL) chopped fresh flat-leaf parsley
1 onion, grated
2 green onions, chopped
2 Tbsp (30 mL) number 2 bulgur
2⅓ cups (580 mL) all-purpose flour
½ tsp (2 mL) baking powder
2½ tsp (12 mL) ground coriander
1 cup (250 mL) canned chickpeas, drained and rinsed
canola oil for cooking

Mix the spinach and salt. Press to extract as much liquid as possible. Reserve the juice.

In a large bowl, add the spinach, parsley, onion, green onions, bulgur, flour, baking powder, coriander and spinach juice. Knead to mix well. Add the chickpeas and mix well.

In a pan on high heat, add the canola oil. With wet hands, take ½ cup (125 mL) of the mixture and flatten into a medium-sized pancake. Fry for 1 minute on each side. Lay on a paper towel to drain well. Make all the pancakes this same way. Serve hot with grape molasses.

Monnamates Southnehs

MAIN DISHES

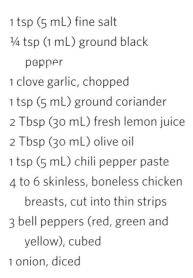

Djedj Flaad

CHICKEN WITH PEPPERS

MARINATING TIME 2 hours   **COOKING TIME** 30 to 45 minutes   **SERVINGS** 4 to 6

1 tsp (5 mL) fine salt

¼ tsp (1 mL) ground black pepper

1 clove garlic, chopped

1 tsp (5 mL) ground coriander

2 Tbsp (30 mL) fresh lemon juice

2 Tbsp (30 mL) olive oil

1 tsp (5 mL) chili pepper paste

4 to 6 skinless, boneless chicken breasts, cut into thin strips

3 bell peppers (red, green and yellow), cubed

1 onion, diced

In a bowl, add the salt, black pepper, garlic, coriander, lemon juice, olive oil and chili pepper paste. Mix well.

In a baking dish, add the chicken and cover well with the marinade. Add the peppers and onions overtop. Cover and leave in the refrigerator for about 2 hours.

Preheat the oven to 350ºC (175ºF). Take the chicken out of the refrigerator and bake for 30 to 45 minutes. Serve with potatoes.

Abbare ma Rez

CAPER STEW

We always enjoy this caper stew, an Easter classic, with undeniable frenzy.
I take time to make a large amount since my family goes crazy for it, especially
my brother, Freddy. To desalt the capers, put them in cool water for 24 hours,
changing the water regularly.

PREPARATION TIME 30 minutes   **COOKING TIME** 1½ hours   **SERVINGS** 4 to 6

2 Tbsp (30 mL) butter

1¼ pounds (625 g) beef or lamb
strip loin, cut into 2-inch
(5 cm) cubes

2 tsp (10 mL) fine salt

1 Tbsp (15 mL) ground allspice

4 Tbsp (60 mL) flour

3 cups (750 mL) water

1 Tbsp (15 mL) dakka, whole in
a spice infuser

1 small onion, quartered

2 pounds (1 kg) capers, desalted
(see recipe introduction)

2 cups (500 mL) verjuice (or
1 cup/250 mL lemon juice)

1 tsp (5 mL) ground dakka

In a large pot, melt and brown the butter on high heat.
Sear the meat for a few minutes until it has colour.
Season with the salt and allspice. Add the flour and mix.
Add the water, attach the spice infuser to the pot and
add the onion. Simmer on low heat for 1 hour. Add the
capers, verjuice and ground dakka. Simmer for another
30 minutes. Serve with rice.

Kibbeh Ndamara

BASIC KIBBEH

Kibbeh is the indispensable base for a number of Middle Eastern dishes, and there are many varieties. To make this recipe more easily, grate the onions in a food processor. Add the bulgur and salt. Run the processor for a few seconds while adding the water and incorporate the meat. Mix with the processor until it all comes together in a ball.

PREPARATION TIME 30 minutes   **YIELD** 24 to 36 balls

1 medium onion, grated
2½ cups (625 mL) number 1 bulgur, rinsed well in cold water
1 tsp (5 mL) fine salt
¾ cup (175 mL) water
1 pound (500 g) habra meat

In a bowl, add the onions, bulgur and salt. Knead, in the bowl, while adding the water gradually. With wet hands, continue to knead, adding the meat gradually until an easily workable dough is obtained. Make little meatballs the size of cherries. Refrigerate or freeze the meatballs to use at another time.

Barzolat Malfoufeh

STEAK ROLLS

PREPARATION TIME 20 minutes   **COOKING TIME** 45 to 60 minutes   **SERVINGS** 4 to 6

1 pound (500 g) filet mignon, sliced thinly

8 cloves garlic, cut in half lengthwise

1 green bell pepper, cut into thin strips

2 tsp (10 mL) fine salt

2 tsp (10 mL) ground dakka

2 Tbsp (30 mL) butter

4 cups (1 L) tomato juice

2 Tbsp (30 mL) tomato paste

On the counter, lay out the slices of the filet mignon. Put 2 halved garlic cloves and one strip of bell pepper on each slice. Season with 1 tsp (5 mL) of the salt and 1 tsp (5 mL) of the dakka. Make a small roll from each piece and use a toothpick to hold the roll together. Set aside.

In a large pan, melt and brown the butter on high heat. Add the rolls and sear for 1 minute on each side. Add the tomato juice and tomato paste. Season with the remaining salt and dakka. Cook on low heat for 45 to 60 minutes. Serve with pasta or rice.

Kneysat ma Rez

RICE-STUFFED MIGNONETTES

PREPARATION TIME 30 minutes **COOKING TIME** 1 hour **SERVINGS** 4 to 6

5 ounces (150 g) lean ground
    beef
½ cup (125 mL) medium-grain
    rice, rinsed well
½ tsp (2 mL) fine salt
1 tsp (5 mL) ground dakka
2 Tbsp (30 mL) pine nuts
10 pieces of filet mignon,
    cut into 2- × 2- × 3-inch
    (5 × 5 × 8 cm) pieces, 3–5 oz
    (90–150 g) each
3 Tbsp (45 mL) butter
4 Tbsp (60 mL) tomato paste
3 cups (750 mL) water

In a bowl, mix the ground beef, rice, salt, dakka and pine nuts. Set aside. Taking a piece of the filet mignon, make a deep incision on one side and widen the opening with your thumb. Stuff with the ground beef and rice mixture and close with a toothpick.

In a large pot on high heat, melt and brown the butter. Sear the stuffed pieces for 1 minute on each side.

In a bowl, dilute the tomato paste with the water. Pour into the pot with the filet mignon. Let simmer on low heat for about 1 hour. Serve with Pomegranate Carrots (page 71) and rice.

Dobbo ma Burghol

ROAST BEEF IN VINEGAR

PREPARATION TIME 10 minutes · **COOKING TIME** 1½ to 2 hours · **SERVINGS** 4 to 6

2 pounds (1 kg) roast sirloin or roast filet mignon

10 cloves garlic, whole, peeled

1 Tbsp (15 mL) fine salt

2 Tbsp (30 mL) ground dakka

½ cup (125 mL) butter

4 cups (1 L) tomato juice

1 cup (250 mL) water

1 tsp (5 mL) fine salt

3 cups (750 mL) red wine vinegar

Lay the roast on a cutting board. With a sharp knife, make 10 incisions here and there in the roast. Stuff with the garlic cloves and season with the salt and 1 Tbsp (15 mL) of the dakka.

In a large pot on medium heat, melt and brown the butter. Sear the stuffed roast for 2 to 3 minutes on each side. Add the tomato juice, water, salt, remaining dakka and vinegar. Cook 1½ to 2 hours, until the roast is tender. Remove from the pot and place on a cutting board. Carve into 1-inch (2.5 cm) slices. Serve with Bulgur or Freekeh (page 101) and the cooking juices.

Jazar bel Reman

POMEGRANATE CARROTS

PREPARATION TIME 15 minutes · **COOKING TIME** 15 to 20 minutes · **SERVINGS** 4 to 6

3 Tbsp (45 mL) butter

6 cups (1.5 L) carrots, peeled and cut finely on the diagonal

2 tsp (10 mL) fine salt

1 Tbsp (15 mL) pomegranate molasses

1 tsp (5 mL) tomato paste

½ cup (125 mL) water

In a pot, melt the butter on low heat. Add the carrots and salt. Cover and cook from 4 to 5 minutes, stirring from time to time so that the carrots do not burn. Add the pomegranate molasses, tomato paste and water. Mix well and let simmer on low heat for 8 to 10 minutes.

Kibbeh Hamiss

LAMB STEW WITH KIBBEH

PREPARATION TIME 15 minutes   **COOKING TIME** 1 hour   **SERVINGS** 4 to 6

3 Tbsp (45 mL) butter

1¼ pounds (625 g) lamb or beef,
    cut into 2-inch (5 cm) cubes

1 Tbsp (15 mL) fine salt

2 Tbsp (30 mL) ground allspice

1 onion, grated finely

8 cups (2 L) water

1 recipe Basic Kibbeh (page 65)

1 tsp (5 mL) ground dakka

VINAIGRETTE

½ cup (125 mL) red wine vinegar

½ tsp (2 mL) puréed garlic

salt to taste

ground Aleppo pepper to taste

In a large pot on high heat, melt and brown the butter. Brown the cubes of meat, about 1 to 2 minutes on each side, until they turn a rich, dark brown. Season with the salt and allspice. Add the onion and brown. Add the water, cover and bring to a boil. Let simmer on low heat for 45 minutes. Add the kibbeh and let simmer for 5 to 10 minutes.

To make the vinaigrette, mix the vinegar, garlic, salt and Aleppo pepper in a bowl. Serve the stew in individual bowls, with vinaigrette overtop each. Accompany with pita bread and radishes.

Kibbeh Mehchiyeh

KIBBEH STUFFED WITH BUTTER

To make this recipe more easily, grate the onions in a food processor. Add the bulgur and salt. Run the processor for a few seconds while adding the water and incorporating the meat. Mix with the processor until it all comes together in a ball. Make Pomegranate Kibbeh (page 75) with these, or make a nice appetizer by barbequing the balls (add a little dried mint to the mixture).

PREPARATION TIME 30 to 45 minutes **SERVINGS** 4 to 6

7 ounces (200 g) cold butter
ground dakka
1 medium onion, grated
2 cups (500 mL) number 1
    bulgur, rinsed well in cold
    water
1 tsp (5 mL) salt
¾ cup (175 mL) water
1 pound (500 g) habra meat

Cut the butter into small cubes, about ½ inch (1 cm) in size, and sprinkle with dakka. Freeze.

In a large bowl, mix the onion, bulgur and salt. Add the water and stir. With wet hands, gradually add the meat, kneading the mixture to obtain a workable dough. Make the meatballs the size of prunes. Place a meatball in the palm of your hand. Stick the index finger of your other hand into the meatball to make a hole from one end to the other without piercing it. Create a well and press lightly. Pivot the kibbeh until it forms an eggcup shape. (See photos.) Put a cube of frozen butter in the cavity and close the opening. Store the stuffed kibbeh in the refrigerator for another time.

Kibbeh Remenyeh

POMEGRANATE KIBBEH

The taste of pomegranate brings back good childhood memories to me. In the fall, when pomegranates were in season, my mother would often prepare a bowl of pomegranate seeds for us to eat once we had returned home from school.

PREPARATION TIME 30 minutes   **COOKING TIME** 1¼ hours   **SERVINGS** 4 to 6

3 Tbsp (45 mL) butter

1 pound (500 g) beef sirloin or lamb, cut into 2-inch (5 cm) cubes

1 onion, finely chopped

1 tsp (5 mL) fine salt

1 tsp (5 mL) ground dakka

2 cups (500 mL) water

1 Tbsp (15 mL) dakka, whole in a spice infuser

4 celery stalks, with their leaves, cut into ¼-inch (6 mm) slices

2 zucchini, cut into 1-inch (2.5 cm) cubes

2 eggplants, cut into 1-inch (2.5 cm) cubes

3 large tomatoes, cut into 1-inch (2.5 cm) cubes

1 Tbsp (15 mL) pomegranate molasses

4 cups (1 L) pomegranate juice

1 tsp (5 mL) ground allspice

1 recipe Kibbeh Stuffed with Butter (page 73)

Melt and brown the butter in a large pot on high heat. Sear the cubes of meat on all sides. Add the onions, salt and dakka. Cook until the onions are transparent. Add the water and attach the spice infuser to the pot. Bring to a boil. Reduce the heat to low and cook for 30 minutes. Add the celery and cook for 15 minutes. Add the zucchini, eggplants, tomatoes, pomegranate molasses and juice, and allspice. Let simmer for 15 to 20 minutes. Add the stuffed kibbeh and simmer for 10 minutes to cook the meatballs. Serve with radishes and pita bread.

Kibbeh Hadde

KIBBEH FLORETS

PREPARATION TIME 90 to 105 minutes   **COOKING TIME** 45 to 60 minutes   **SERVINGS** 4 to 6

½ cup (125 mL) butter

3 medium onions, diced

1 tsp (5 mL) fine salt

1 tsp (5 mL) ground dakka

1 Tbsp (15 mL) chili pepper paste

1 cup (250 mL) walnuts,
    chopped roughly

¼ cup (60 mL) sesame seeds
    (optional)

1 tsp (5 mL) ground cumin
    (optional)

1 recipe Basic Kibbeh (page 65)

walnuts, cut in half, and
    pistachios or pine nuts

In a large pot, melt the butter on medium heat. Add the onions, salt, dakka, chili pepper paste and walnuts, and the sesame seeds and cumin (if using). Mix. Cook for 5 minutes. Remove from the heat. Cool in the refrigerator for 1 hour.

Taking a Basic Kibbeh meatball, place a ball in the palm of your hand. (See photos page 73.) Stick the index finger of your other hand into the ball to make a hole from one end to the other without piercing it. Create a well and press lightly. Pivot the kibbeh until it forms an eggcup shape. Put 1 tsp (5 mL) of the stuffing in the cavity.

Arrange the stuffed kibbeh in a greased baking dish. Decorate with the walnuts, pistachios and pine nuts. Preheat the oven to 350°F (175°C). Bake the stuffed kibbeh for 45 to 60 minutes. Serve with a salad of your choice.

Kibbeh bel Seniyeh

KIBBEH ON A PLATTER

This delicious kibbeh dish can be made with either a meat or a butter stuffing.

PREPARATION TIME 90 minutes   **COOKING TIME** 45 to 60 minutes   **SERVINGS** 4 to 6

MEAT STUFFING

3 Tbsp (45 mL) butter

1½ pounds (750 g) lean ground
   beef

2 onions, diced

1 tsp (5 mL) fine salt

2 tsp (10 mL) ground dakka

1 tsp (5 mL) ground allspice

1 cup (250 mL) walnuts,
   chopped roughly

¼ cup (60 mL) pine nuts
   (optional)

MAIN

1 recipe Basic Kibbeh (page 65)

butter knobs

olive oil

BUTTER STUFFING (VARIATION)

3 onions, diced

7 ounces (200 g) butter

1 tsp (5 mL) fine salt

2 tsp (10 mL) ground dakka

½ cup (125 mL) walnuts,
   chopped roughly

MEAT STUFFING | In a large pot, melt and brown the butter on high heat. Sear the meat, making sure to break it up well. Add the onions, salt, dakka and allspice. Mix well and cook for about 10 minutes. Add the walnuts and the pine nuts (if using). Remove from heat. Let cool in the refrigerator for about 1 hour. (This part of the recipe can be made the night before.)

MAIN | Butter a baking dish. Divide the Basic Kibbeh into two halves and set one half aside. With wet hands, take a prune-sized amount of the kibbeh and flatten it between your palms, making it as thin as possible. Put this flattened disc in the baking dish. Repeat with the rest of the one-half of the kibbeh to entirely cover the bottom of the dish. Take the stuffing and spread it all overtop the bottom layer of kibbeh discs. Take the remaining kibbeh and make discs, placing them in a layer overtop the stuffing. Smooth out the layers so that they are level and make sure not to leave gaps. Press the layers down firmly with the palms of wet hands. **(CONTINUED ON PAGE 80)**

KIBBEH ON A PLATTER (CONTINUED FROM PAGE 78)

With a sharp knife dipped in water, score the top to make a diamond-and-grid pattern. (See photos.) Preheat the oven to 350°F (175°C). Dot the top with knobs of butter and sprinkle with olive oil. Bake in the oven for 45 to 60 minutes. Serve with a salad of your choice, or yogurt.

BUTTER STUFFING (VARIATION) | In a large pot, sauté the onions, butter, salt and dakka for 2 minutes. Add the walnuts and cook for 3 minutes. Remove from heat and let cool in the refrigerator for 1 hour. (This part of the recipe can be made the night before.)

Makaronneh bel Fourn

BAKED SPAGHETTI

This is another recipe the members of my family have carefully passed down for many generations. Everyone volunteers when it is time to eat the leftovers.

PREPARATION TIME 30 minutes   **COOKING TIME** 2 hours   **SERVINGS** 6 to 8

½ cup (125 mL) butter

13 ounces (400 g) lean ground beef

1 Tbsp (15 mL) fine salt

2 Tbsp (30 mL) ground allspice

6 cups (1.5 L) tomato juice

½ cup (125 mL) tomato paste

2 pounds (1 kg) spaghetti

In a pot, melt the butter on high heat until lightly browned. Sear the meat, making sure to break it up well. Cook for 2 to 3 minutes. Season with the salt and allspice. Add the tomato juice and paste. Bring to a boil and let simmer on low heat for 30 minutes.

Cook the spaghetti according to the package instructions. Drain well. Preheat the oven to 350°F (175°C).

Put the cooked spaghetti into 2 baking dishes, cover with the sauce and mix well. Bake in the oven for 1 to 1½ hours, until the top is golden brown. Serve with a mixed green salad.

Yabrak el Laghana

CABBAGE CIGARS

PREPARATION TIME 30 minutes **COOKING TIME** 2 hours **SERVINGS** 4 to 6

1 white cabbage

1½ cups (375 mL) medium-grain rice

1½ cups (375 mL) lean ground beef

1 tsp (5 mL) fine salt

1 Tbsp (15 mL) ground allspice

5 Tbsp (75 mL) tomato paste

3 cups (750 mL) water

¼ cup (60 mL) pomegranate molasses

1 tsp (5 mL) fine salt

2 tsp (10 mL) puréed garlic

4 tsp (20 mL) dried mint

ground Aleppo pepper to taste

Taking the cabbage head, cut off the root end and outermost leaves and discard. Cut the large outer leaves off. (Keep the inner leaves and core for another time.) Blanch the outer leaves in a pot of salted boiling water. Drain and let cool. Cut in half, remove the hard middle part and set aside.

In a bowl, add the rice, meat, salt, allspice and 2 Tbsp (30 mL) of the tomato paste and mix well. Lay a leaf on the counter and place 2 Tbsp (30 mL) of the stuffing on one half. Close the ends and roll up, making a cigar shape, fastening with a toothpick. Repeat until all the stuffing has been used. Keep remaining leaves for another time.

In a large pot, arrange the hard middle parts of the leaves in a layer. Arrange the cabbage cigars in a circle in a layer overtop. In a bowl, add the water, pomegranate molasses, the rest of the tomato paste and the salt, and mix. Pour into the pot. Place a large plate overtop the cigars to keep them in place during cooking. Cook on medium heat for 45 to 60 minutes.

Remove about ½ cup (125 mL) of the cooking liquid. In a bowl, add the cooking liquid, garlic and mint, and mix. Pour back into the pot. Let simmer for 10 minutes. Remove the plate. Lift the cigars out of the pot and arrange on a platter. Sprinkle with Aleppo pepper to your liking and serve.

Mushroom bel Lahmeh

FILET MIGNON WITH MUSHROOMS

In Aleppo, my mother would prepare this dish with truffles. Since truffles are expensive and sometimes difficult to source, I've replaced them with mushrooms.

MARINATING TIME 12 to 24 hours **COOKING TIME** 35 minutes **SERVINGS** 4 to 6

10 ounces (300 g) beef filet mignon, cut into ½- to ¾-inch (1–2 cm) cubes

2 Tbsp (30 mL) olive oil

1 tsp (5 mL) fine salt

2 tsp (10 mL) ground allspice

3 Tbsp (45 mL) butter

1½ pounds (750 g) mushrooms, sliced

1 cup (250 mL) water

In a large bowl, mix the cubed meat, olive oil, salt and allspice. Let marinate for 12 to 24 hours in the refrigerator.

In a large pan, brown the butter. Sear the cubes of meat with the marinade for about 1 minute on each side. Add the mushrooms and mix. Add the water, bring to a boil and let simmer on low heat for 30 minutes. Serve with rice and green vegetables.

Kabbab fladd

KEBOBS WITH RED BELL PEPPERS

PREPARATION TIME 30 minutes   **COOKING TIME** 25 minutes   **SERVINGS** 4 to 6

1¼ pounds (625 g) lean ground
  beef
1 tsp (5 mL) ground dakka
1 Tbsp (15 mL) fine salt
3 Tbsp (45 mL) butter
2 Tbsp (30 mL) olive oil
2 onions, diced finely
6 cups (1.5 L) cubed red bell
  pepper
1 cup (250 mL) (or to taste)
  cubed chili pepper
2 tomatoes, cubed (optional)
1 tsp (5 mL) fine salt
1 Tbsp (15 mL) pomegranate
  molasses
pita bread cut into triangles
fresh parsley, chopped
pine nuts, toasted

In a large bowl, mix the meat, dakka and salt. Make cherry-sized meatballs.

In a large pan on high heat, melt and brown the butter. Add the meatballs and brown for 2 to 3 minutes. Set aside.

In a large pot, heat the olive oil on medium heat. Add the onions and cook until they are transparent. Add the cubed bell pepper and chili pepper and sauté for 5 minutes. Add the tomatoes, salt and pomegranate molasses. Let simmer on low heat for about 10 minutes. Add the browned meatballs and let simmer for 5 minutes. To serve, arrange the pita bread triangles on a serving plate. Add the kebobs and sauce in the middle of the plate. Garnish to your liking with chopped parsley and toasted pine nuts.

Kabbab bel Bourghol

KEBOBS WITH BULGUR

This dish is very easy to prepare and is ideal for week nights. My children like to eat it with ketchup. In winter, nothing is more comforting than to serve it with a good soup.

PREPARATION TIME 15 minutes   **COOKING TIME** 15 to 20 minutes   **SERVINGS** 4 to 6

1 pound (500 g) lean ground beef
1 onion, grated
1 cup (250 mL) number 1 bulgur, rinsed well in cold water
1 tsp (5 mL) fine salt
1 tsp (5 mL) ground dakka
1 tsp (5 mL) ground cumin
1 tsp (5 mL) ground coriander
2 tsp (10 mL) dried mint
½ cup (125 mL) butter
2 Tbsp (30 mL) canola oil

In a large bowl, add the meat, onions, bulgur, salt, dakka, cumin, coriander and mint. Mix well. With the mixture, make 2- to 3-inch (5–8 cm) pancakes about ½ inch (1 cm) thick.

In a large pan on high heat, add the butter and canola oil and cook until the butter is melted and browned. Cook the pancake kebobs for 1 minute on each side. Serve hot with a salad or soup.

Kabbab bel Laban

KEBOBS WITH YOGURT

PREPARATION TIME 15 minutes **COOKING TIME** 10 minutes **SERVINGS** 4 to 6

1 pound (500 g) lean ground
    beef
1 tsp (5 mL) fine salt
1 tsp (5 mL) ground dakka
1 Tbsp (15 mL) butter
2 cups (500 mL) yogurt
1 tsp (5 mL) garlic, chopped
1 Tbsp (15 mL) cornstarch
1 tsp (5 mL) salt
pita bread, cut into triangles
4 eggs, cooked sunny-side up
    (optional)
fresh parsley, chopped
pine nuts, toasted

In a large bowl, mix the meat, salt and dakka. Make cherry-sized meatballs.

In a large pan on high heat, melt and brown the butter. Add the meatballs and brown for 2 to 3 minutes.

In a medium pot, on low heat, add the yogurt, garlic, cornstarch and salt. Mix well and cook for 5 minutes, stirring often. To serve, arrange the pita bread triangles on a serving plate. Pour the hot yogurt overtop. Add the meatballs and the cooked eggs, if using. Garnish to your liking with chopped parsley and toasted pine nuts.

Kabbab bel Karaz

KEBOBS WITH CHERRIES

I serve this extremely delicious dish for family weekend festivities. Use Aleppo cherries for the sour cherries, if you can find them; if not, use Morello cherries.

PREPARATION TIME 30 minutes   **COOKING TIME** 3½ hours   **SERVINGS** 4 to 6

four 19-ounce (540 mL) cans pitted sour cherries, with their juice
6 Tbsp (90 mL) granulated sugar
4 Tbsp (60 mL) fresh lemon juice
1½ pounds (750 g) lean ground beef
1 Tbsp (15 mL) ground dakka
1 tsp (5 mL) fine salt
3 Tbsp (45 mL) butter
¼ cup (60 mL) dried breadcrumbs
1 cup (250 mL) frozen cherries (optional)
pita bread cut into triangles
¼ cup (60 mL) fresh parsley, finely chopped
3 Tbsp (45 mL) pine nuts, toasted
ground cinnamon to taste

In a large pot, bring the sour cherries and their juice, the sugar and the lemon juice to a boil. Let simmer on low heat for 2½ to 3 hours, until the mixture has reduced by a third.

In a large shallow bowl, mix the meat, 2 tsp (10 mL) of the dakka and the salt. Make cherry-sized meatballs.

In a large pot on high heat, melt and brown the butter. Add the meatballs and brown for about 2 to 3 minutes. Add the breadcrumbs and the remaining 1 tsp (5 mL) of dakka. Stir for 1 minute. Add the cherry reduction and frozen cherries (if using). Mix well. Turn the heat to low and simmer for 10 minutes.

Warm the pita bread in a pan in the oven. To serve, arrange the pita bread triangles on a serving plate. Add the kebobs in the middle of the plate. Garnish to your liking with chopped parsley, toasted pine nuts and ground cinnamon.

KEBOBS WITH SPINACH

PREPARATION TIME 30 minutes **COOKING TIME** 15 to 30 minutes **SERVINGS** 4 to 6

1¼ pounds (625 g) lean ground beef

1 tsp (5 mL) fine salt

1 tsp (5 mL) ground dakka

2 Tbsp (30 mL) butter

1 onion, sliced thinly

1 Tbsp (15 mL) puréed garlic

1 Tbsp (15 mL) ground coriander

2 pounds (1 kg) spinach, washed and stalks removed

Put the meat in a large bowl and season with the salt and dakka. Mix well. Make cherry-sized meatballs.

In a large pot, melt and brown the butter. Brown the meatballs for 2 to 3 minutes. Add the onions and cook until transparent. Add the garlic, coriander and spinach. Mix well and cook on low heat for 5 to 10 minutes. Serve on a bed of rice. Accompany with fresh lemon juice and yogurt.

Rez
RICE

PREPARATION TIME 5 minutes   **COOKING TIME** 20 to 25 minutes   **SERVINGS** 4 to 6

3 Tbsp (45 mL) butter

1½ cups (375 mL) long-grain rice, rinsed well

1 tsp (5 mL) fine salt

3¼ cups (810 mL) boiling water

In a pot on high heat, add the butter. Add the rice and toast for 1 minute. Add the salt and water. Cover and cook on low heat for 20 to 25 minutes.

Rez bi' Chareriyeh
RICE WITH VERMICELLI

PREPARATION TIME 10 minutes   **COOKING TIME** 30 minutes   **SERVINGS** 4 to 6

3 Tbsp (45 mL) butter

¼ cup (60 mL) vermicelli noodles

1 cup (250 mL) long-grain rice, rinsed well

2¼ cups (560 mL) water

½ tsp (2 mL) fine salt

In a pot, melt the butter on high heat and brown the vermicelli. Add the rice and stir for a few seconds. Add the water and salt. Bring to a boil, cover and cook on low heat for 25 to 30 minutes.

Fatet el Djedj

YOGURT CHICKEN

I use leftovers for this recipe.

PREPARATION TIME 15 minutes   **COOKING TIME** 40 minutes   **SERVINGS** 4 to 6

2 cups (500 mL) long-grain rice, cooked

2 cups (500 mL) cooked chicken, cubed

3 cups (750 mL) yogurt

1 Tbsp (15 mL) cornstarch

2 tsp (10 mL) puréed garlic

½ tsp (2 mL) fine salt

1 Tbsp (15 mL) butter

¼ cup (60 mL) pine nuts

Preheat the oven to 350°F (175°C). In a large baking dish, spread a thin layer of the cooked rice. Add the cooked chicken cubes. Cover and bake for 30 minutes.

In a pot on low heat, add the yogurt, cornstarch, garlic and salt. Stir. Warm for 8 to 10 minutes.

In a pan, melt the butter on medium heat. Add the pine nuts. Brown until golden-coloured. Set aside.

Take the chicken out of the oven and remove the cover. Top with the warm yogurt mixture. Serve hot, with pieces of pita bread and pine nuts.

Hachweh Diet

CHESTNUT STUFFING

This stuffing is an excellant accompaniment to poultry or another main dish such as Roasted Leg of Lamb (see page 101).

PREPARATION TIME 30 minutes   **COOKING TIME** 45 to 60 minutes   **SERVINGS** 4 to 6

RICE

2 Tbsp (30 mL) butter

1½ cups (375 mL) long-grain rice, rinsed well

3 cups (750 mL) chicken stock

½ tsp (2 mL) fine salt

MEAT

1 Tbsp (15 mL) butter

1 pound (500 g) lean ground beef

½ tsp (2 mL) fine salt

2 tsp (10 mL) ground dakka

½ cup (125 mL) chicken stock

NUTS

20 chestnuts

3 Tbsp (45 mL) butter

¾ cup (185 mL) blanched almonds

¼ cup (60 mL) pine nuts

RICE | In a large pot over high heat, melt and brown the butter. Add the rice ane brown for 2 minutes. Add the chicken stock and salt. Reduce the heat to very low, and cover and simmer for about 20 minutes, or until the rice has absorbed the liquid. Set aside.

MEAT | In a large pot over high heat, melt and brown the butter. Add the meat and brown, stirring to break it up well. Add the salt and dakka and cook for 3 minutes. Reduce the heat to low, add the chicken stock and simmer for 10 minutes. Set aside.

NUTS | Use a sharp knife to cut an × into the top of each chestnut. Put about 10 chestnuts in the microwave and cook for 3 minutes on high. Repeat with the remaining chestnuts. Let cool. Peel. In a large pan over high heat, melt the butter. Add the chestnuts and toast, stirring, until golden-coloured, about 1 minute. Set aside. In the same pan, add the almonds and toast for 2 to 3 minutes, stirring. Set aside. In the same pan, add the pine nuts and toast for 1 to 2 minutes, stirring.

In a large bowl, combine the rice, meat and toasted nuts. Serve alongside a main dish.

Djehje Mhchiyeh
STUFFED CHICKEN

If you are cooking a turkey instead of a chicken, double this recipe and extend the cooking time for about 2 to 3 hours, depending on the size of the turkey.

PREPARATION TIME 15 to 30 minutes   **COOKING TIME** 1½ hours   **SERVINGS** 4 to 6

¼ cup (60 mL) long-grain rice, cooked

4 ounces (125 g) lean ground beef

½ tsp (2 mL) fine salt

½ tsp (2 mL) ground dakka

1 Tbsp (15 mL) pine nuts, toasted

3 Tbsp (45 mL) blanched almonds, toasted

1 whole medium chicken

1 tsp (5 mL) fine salt

1 tsp (5 mL) ground allspice

¼ cup (60 mL) olive oil

½ cup (125 mL) water

Preheat the oven to 350ºC (175ºF). In a large bowl, mix the rice, beef, salt, dakka, pine nuts and almonds. Set aside.

Rinse the chicken under cold water and pat dry with paper towels. Place in a broiler. Coat the inside and outside of the bird with the salt, allspice and olive oil. Stuff the chicken with the stuffing. Pour water into the bottom of the broiler. (You can add 2 cups/500 mL small carrots and a dozen baby potatoes to the broiler at this point, to cook with the chicken.) Cover and cook in the oven for 1 hour. Remove the cover. Continue to cook in the oven for 30 more minutes.

Put the chicken and cooked vegetables in a serving dish. Strain the cooking liquid from the broiler and reserve for another use, if desired. Serve with rice and a green salad.

Djedj bel Zetonne
CHICKEN WITH OLIVES

PREPARATION TIME 15 to 30 minutes **COOKING TIME** 45 minutes **SERVINGS** 4 to 6

3 Tbsp (45 mL) butter
1 Tbsp (15 mL) olive oil
1¼ pounds (625 g) skinless, boneless chicken breasts, cut into strips
1 onion, diced
1 tsp (5 mL) fine salt
1 tsp (5 mL) ground allspice
½ cup (125 mL) white wine
3 Tbsp (45 mL) fresh lemon juice
1 pound (500 g) pitted green olives
1 cup (250 mL) water
1 baguette, cut into 1-inch (2.5 cm) slices on the diagonal
fresh parsley, chopped

In a large pot, melt and brown the butter and olive oil. Sear the strips of chicken for 1 minute on each side. Add the onions and season with the salt and allspice. Cook, stirring, until the onions are tender. Add the wine, lemon juice, olives and water. Let simmer on low heat for 25 to 30 minutes.

Preheat the oven to 350°F (175°C). Put the baguette slices into an ovenproof serving dish. Heat the baguette pieces in the oven for 5 minutes, until they are crusty. Take out of the oven and cover with the chicken mixture. Garnish with chopped parsley and serve with a salad of your choice.

Martadella Mehchyeh

STUFFED ROLL ON A BED OF CAPERS

When August arrives, we pick unripe grapes from the vines at the end of my yard. We then use a juice extractor to get the verjuice that I use in many of these recipes. Before you use the capers, soak them in fresh water for 24 hours, changing the water regularly.

PREPARATION TIME 20 minutes   **COOKING TIME** 1 hour   **SERVINGS** 4 to 6

3½ ounces (100 g) lean ground beef

⅓ cup (80 mL) medium-grain rice, well rinsed

½ tsp (2 mL) fine salt

1 tsp (5 mL) ground dakka

2 Tbsp (30 mL) pine nuts

¼ cup (60 mL) red bell pepper, diced very fine

1 pound (500 g) habra meat

½ tsp (2 mL) fine salt

1 tsp (5 mL) ground dakka

¼ cup (60 mL) breadcrumbs

3 Tbsp (45 mL) butter

2 pounds (1 kg) capers, desalted

4 cups (1 L) water

1 cup (250 mL) verjuice (or ½ cup/125 mL fresh lemon juice)

In a large bowl, mix the ground beef, rice, salt, dakka, pine nuts and bell peppers. Set aside.

In a large bowl, mix the habra meat, salt, dakka and breadcrumbs. On a flat surface, spread the habra meat mixture in a rectangle about 12×8 inches (30×20 cm). With the ground beef mixture, make a long, thin sausage. Place lengthwise in the middle of the habra meat rectangle. Roll up the rectangle, enclosing the sausage. With wet hands, close the edge of the roll. (See photos.)

In a pan, melt and brown the butter on high heat. Add the sausage roll and sear until cooked through. Add the capers, water and verjuice. Let simmer on low heat for 1 hour. Cut the roll into slices. Serve hot with rice.

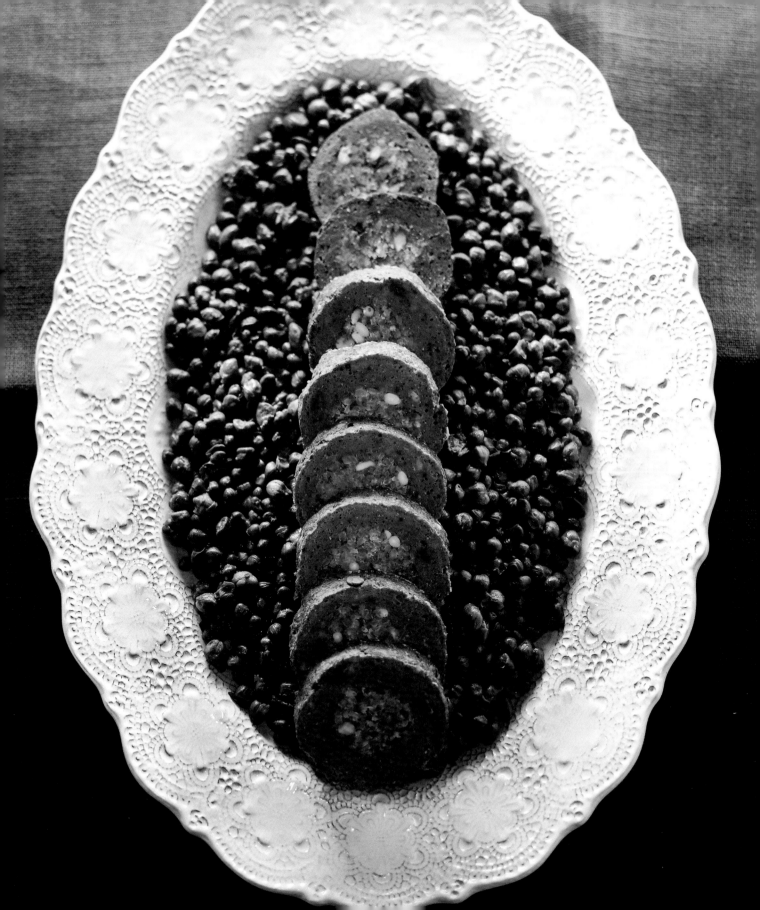

Faghdeh bel Fourn
ROASTED LEG OF LAMB

PREPARATION TIME 10 minutes **COOKING TIME** 2 to 3 hours **SERVINGS** 4 to 6

1 onion, grated

1 tsp (5 mL) fine salt

1 tsp (5 mL) ground dakka

1 leg of lamb, 3 pounds (1.5 kg)

1 cup (250 mL) water or wine, or
   half water and half wine

Preheat the oven to 500°F (260°C). In a bowl, mix the onions, salt and dakka. Set aside. Rinse the lamb in cold water and pat dry with paper towels. Put into a broiler. Coat with the onion mixture and add the liquid. Cook in the oven uncovered for 30 minutes. Reduce the heat to 350°F (175°C), cover and cook for 1½ hours. Increase the heat to 500°F (260°C), remove the cover and cook for 15 to 30 minutes more to obtain a nicely golden-coloured leg of lamb. Serve with Bulgur or Freekeh (below) or Chestnut Stuffing (page 94), both pictured here.

Bourghol ma Freekeh
BULGUR OR FREEKEH

PREPARATION TIME 5 minutes **COOKING TIME** 25 minutes **SERVINGS** 4 to 6

1½ cups (375 mL) number 3
   bulgur, or freekeh

4 Tbsp (60 mL) butter

1 tsp (5 mL) fine salt

3 cups (750 mL) water (if using
   bulgur) or chicken stock (if
   using freekeh), boiling

In a pot on high heat, brown the bulgur or freekeh in the butter for 1 minute. Add the salt and the boiling water or stock. Cover and cook on low heat for 20 to 25 minutes.

Erman ma Rez

LAMB WITH YOGURT

PREPARATION TIME 10 minutes   **COOKING TIME** 1½ hours   **SERVINGS** 4 to 6

3 Tbsp (45 mL) butter

2 pounds (1 kg) lamb, cut into
4-inch (10 cm) cubes

1 Tbsp (15 mL) fine salt

1 tsp (5 mL) ground allspice

1 tsp (5 mL) ground dakka

1 small onion, cut into quarters

3 cups (750 mL) water

4 cups (1 L) yogurt

1½ Tbsp (22 mL) cornstarch

In a large pot on high heat, melt and brown the butter. Sear the cubed lamb for 1 minute on each side. Add 2 tsp (10 mL) of the salt and the allspice and dakka. Add the onions and water. Cover and let simmer on low heat for 1½ hours.

In a medium bowl, mix the yogurt and cornstarch and the remaining 1 tsp (5 mL) of salt. Add to the lamb and mix well. Increase the heat to medium. As soon as the liquid begins to boil, remove the pot from heat. Serve the lamb with Rice (page 91) or Bulgur or Freekeh (page 101).

Samak' bel Fourn

BAKED TILAPIA

PREPARATION TIME 10 minutes **COOKING TIME** 20 to 25 minutes **SERVINGS** 4 to 6

1 tsp (5 mL) fine salt

¼ tsp (1 mL) ground black
  pepper

1 clove garlic, chopped

1 tsp (5 mL) ground coriander

2 Tbsp (30 mL) fresh lemon juice

4 Tbsp (60 mL) olive oil

1 tsp (5 mL) chili pepper paste

4 to 6 tilapia or red snapper
  filets

Preheat the oven to 350°F (175°C). In a baking dish, mix the salt, black pepper, garlic, coriander, lemon juice, olive oil and chili pepper paste. Place the filets in the dish and spoon the marinade overtop to cover well. Bake for 20 to 25 minutes.

Samak' Mekly

FRIED FILET OF SOLE

PREPARATION TIME 10 minutes **COOKING TIME** 5 minutes **SERVINGS** 4

2 eggs, beaten

1 tsp (5 mL) coriander seeds,
  ground

1 tsp (5 mL) fine salt

½ tsp (2 mL) ground allspice

2 cloves garlic, crushed and
  puréed

¼ cup (60 mL) flour

4 sole filets, fresh

1 cup (250 mL) breadcrumbs

2 tsp (10 mL) butter

2 tsp (10 mL) olive oil

In a bowl, mix the eggs, coriander, salt, allspice and garlic. Set aside. Flour the sole filets and dip them into the beaten eggs. Put them into the breadcrumbs and cover them uniformly on both sides. In a large pan, melt and brown the butter and olive oil on high heat. Cook the filets for 1 to 2 minutes on each side. Serve with lemon and vegetables of your choice.

Samat' bel Fourn

BAKED GROUPER

Fresh fish should have red and wet gills, full, shiny eyes and taut, glistening skin. The flesh should be firm and spring back immediately to its original form after being pressed with a finger. This is a complete dish since it has fish, potatoes and tomatoes.

PREPARATION TIME 10 to 15 minutes   **COOKING TIME** 45 to 60 minutes   **SERVINGS** 4 to 6

1 to 2 pounds (500 g–1 kg) whole grouper or walleye, fresh, scaled and gutted

½ cup (125 mL) olive oil

1 tsp (5 mL) tomato paste

1 tsp (5 mL) ground allspice

1 tsp (5 mL) fine salt

3 potatoes, sliced

10 cloves of garlic, whole

1 onion, shaved thinly

2 tomatoes, sliced

Preheat the oven to 350°F (175°C). Rinse the grouper with cold water and pat dry with paper towels. Set aside.

In a bowl, mix the olive oil, tomato paste, allspice and salt. Set aside.

Cut a large sheet of aluminum foil and place it on a baking sheet. Place the fish on the aluminum foil in the centre of the baking sheet. Brush the interior and exterior of the fish with the marinade. Arrange the potatoes, garlic, onions and tomatoes overtop and around the fish. Pour the remaining marinade overtop. Bring the ends of the aluminum foil together, enclosing the fish, vegetables and marinade. Bake for 45 to 60 minutes.

Mechwi

BARBEQUE

Kabbab Mechwi

SKEWERED KEBOBS

With the arrival of winter, we ready the charcoal barbeque every Saturday night in the living room fireplace. If there are leftover skewered kebobs, reheat them by simmering them for a few minutes with a mixture of 1 diced onion, 2 to 3 diced tomatoes, 3 Tbsp (45 mL) olive oil and 1 Tbsp (15 mL) tomato paste.

PREPARATION TIME 30 minutes   **COOKING TIME** 15 to 30 minutes   **SERVINGS** 4 to 6

1 Tbsp (15 mL) fine salt
1½ Tbsp (22 mL) ground dakka
1 tsp (5 mL) ground Aleppo
   pepper or chili pepper paste
   (optional)
1 Tbsp (15 mL) tomato paste
½ cup (125 mL) breadcrumbs
2 pounds (1 kg) lean ground beef
15 to 18 skewers
vegetable oil for grilling

Preheat the barbeque. In a bowl, mix the salt, dakka, Aleppo pepper or chili pepper paste (if using), tomato paste and breadcrumbs. Add the meat and mix well. Make meatballs. Taking a meatball, thread it onto a skewer. Stretch and press the meatball onto the skewer so that it sticks well. Repeat until all the meat mixture is used.

Brush a preheated grill with vegetable oil. Place the skewered kebobs on the barbeque and grill for about 2 minutes on each side, until cooked to your liking. Serve with Parsley Salad and Barbequed Tomatoes (both page 110), both pictured here.

Behmazze

PARSLEY SALAD

PREPARATION TIME 15 minutes **SERVINGS** 4 to 6

3 cups (750 mL) fresh flat-leaf
  parsley, chopped roughly
2 onions, sliced very finely
3 Tbsp (45 mL) ground sumac
1 tsp (5 mL) fine salt
2 Tbsp (30 mL) fresh lemon juice

In a large bowl, add the parsley and onions. Mix. Add the sumac, salt and lemon juice. Mix well. Serve with Skewered Kebobs (see recipe and photo on pages 108–109).

Banadora Mechmiyeh

BARBEQUED TOMATOES

PREPARATION TIME 10 minutes **COOKING TIME** 30 to 40 minutes **SERVINGS** 4 to 6

6 whole, ripe plum tomatoes
1 tsp (5 mL) fine salt
1 tsp (5 mL) chili pepper paste

Preheat the barbeque. With a fork, pierce the tomatoes a few times. Cook on the grill, turning from time to time, until the skins pull off easily. Remove the skins and, with a fork, lightly press the tomatoes to remove the water. Cut the tomatoes into small pieces. Put the tomato pieces into a bowl. Add the salt and chili pepper paste and stir gently to combine. Spread on small pita breads grilled on the barbeque. Serve with Skewered Kebobs (see recipe and photo on pages 108–109).

FILET MIGNON SKEWERS

The word *mechwi* means whole or on skewers, cooked over coals or a wood fire. My family, myself included, always use a charcoal barbeque, which gives such good flavour to a mixed-grill dish. This dish is marinated skewers of meat as well as skewers of onions. You might want to add artichokes to the onion skewers—cut a dozen cleaned artichokes in half, marinate them along with the meat and thread them onto the onion skewers, alternating with the onions.

To serve these skewers as sandwiches, cut a pita bread in half. Open up the sides and brush with the marinade. Grill for a few seconds on the barbeque. Stuff with the cubes of grilled meat and the vegetables.

MARINATING TIME 12 to 24 hours   **COOKING TIME** 30 minutes   **SERVINGS** 4 to 6

1 cup (250 mL) olive oil

2 tsp (10 mL) fine salt

2 tsp (10 mL) ground allspice

1 Tbsp (15 mL) ground Aleppo pepper or chili pepper paste (optional)

2 pounds (1 kg) filet mignon cut into 1½-inch (4 cm) cubes

20 small whole onions, peeled, with roots left intact

In a bowl, mix the olive oil, salt, allspice and Aleppo pepper or chili pepper paste (if using). Add the cubes of meat and mix well. Cover tightly and let marinate for 12 to 24 hours in the refrigerator.

Preheat the barbeque and oil the grill well. Take the meat out of the marinade. Reserve the marinade. Thread the meat onto skewers. Thread the onions onto skewers. (Do not thread the onions onto the same skewers as the meat since the cooking time for each is different.) Cook the skewers on the grill to your liking. Serve with a green salad and Kibbeh Tartar (page 32).

Kabbab bel Banjan

KEBOBS AND EGGPLANT

PREPARATION TIME 15 to 45 minutes **COOKING TIME** 30 to 45 minutes **SERVINGS** 4 to 6

12 long, narrow eggplants

1½ pounds (750 g) ground lamb
or lean ground beef

2 tsp (10 mL) ground dakka

2 tsp (10 mL) fine salt

With a vegetable peeler, peel the eggplants lengthwise in strips, leaving strips of skin between each peeled strip. Then cut the eggplants into rounds 1½ to 2 inches (4–5 cm) thick. Set aside.

In a bowl, mix the meat, dakka and salt. Preheat the barbeque. Oil the grill well with vegetable oil. Make little meatballs about the same size as the eggplant rounds. Skewer the eggplant rounds and meatballs alternately onto the skewers, slightly flattening the meatballs between the eggplant slices as you do so. Grill for 8 to 10 minutes on each side, until the eggplant is tender. Serve hot with pita and bell peppers or hot peppers.

For a softer flavour, precook the eggplant and meatball skewers on the barbeque. Remove the eggplant rounds and meatballs from the skewers and arrange them on a buttered baking dish. Dot with butter. Add ½ cup (125 mL) of water. Cover and bake in the oven at 350°F (175°C) for 30 to 45 minutes.

Shish Taouk

CHICKEN SHISH KEBOB

MARINATING TIME 12 to 24 hours   **COOKING TIME** 25 to 30 minutes   **SERVINGS** 4 to 6

1½ pounds (750 g) skinless, boneless chicken breasts

1 cup (250 mL) mayonnaise

½ cup (125 mL) yogurt

1½ Tbsp (22 mL) fresh lemon juice

1 tsp (5 mL) puréed garlic

1 tsp (5 mL) fine salt

¼ tsp (1 mL) ground black pepper

Cut the chicken breasts into 1½- to 2-inch (4–5 cm) cubes. Set aside.

In a bowl, mix the mayonnaise, yogurt, lemon juice, garlic, salt and pepper. Add the chicken and mix well. Cover and let marinate in the refrigerator for 12 to 24 hours.

Preheat the barbeque. Brush the grill with vegetable oil. Thread the chicken cubes onto skewers, leaving a small space between pieces. Cook on the barbeque for 4 to 5 minutes on each side, until the chicken is cooked through. Serve with Garlic Mayonnaise (page 117).

Djebneh Mhamara

GRILLED PITA WITH CHEESE

Use cheese that has been cubed and stored in brine. Syrian cheese is best when consumed fresh, only a few days old.

PREPARATION TIME 5 minutes   **COOKING TIME** 5 minutes   **SERVINGS** 2

4 ounces (125 g) Syrian cheese, cut into 2-inch (5 cm) cubes
¼ tsp (1 mL) ground Aleppo pepper
¼ tsp (1 mL) olive oil
¼ tsp (1 mL) dried mint, or a few fresh mint leaves, chopped
one 9-inch (23 cm) pita bread

Preheat the barbeque. In a bowl, mix the cubed cheese, Aleppo pepper, olive oil and mint. Slice partway along the edge of the pita and open a pocket into the pita. Stuff the pita pocket with the cheese mixture. Grill on the barbeque for 1 to 2 minutes on each side. Cut into 4 and serve.

Mayonnaise bel Toum

GARLIC MAYONNAISE

This mayonnaise accompanies fries and sandwiches very well. It keeps in the refrigerator for three to four months.

PREPARATION TIME 10 minutes   **YIELD** about 2 cups (500 mL)

1½ tsp (7 mL) puréed garlic
1 tsp (5 mL) salt
1 egg
1 tsp (5 mL) granulated sugar
1 tsp (5 mL) white vinegar
1 cup (250 mL) + 6 Tbsp (90 mL) canola oil

In a food processor, mix the garlic, salt, egg, sugar and vinegar until the mixture has a frothy consistency. Very slowly, pour the canola oil in a thin stream through the opening of the food processor's lid while mixing at high speed.

Djedj Mechwi

BARBEQUED CHICKEN

MARINATING TIME 12 to 24 hours **COOKING TIME** 30 to 40 minutes **SERVINGS** 4 to 6

¼ cup (60 mL) fresh lemon juice

½ cup (125 mL) olive oil

2 tsp (10 mL) fine salt

¼ tsp (1 mL) ground black pepper

½ tsp (2 mL) ground Aleppo pepper

1 chicken cut into 8 pieces (or 3 chicken breasts and 3 chicken thighs, skin on, bone in)

In a bowl, mix the lemon juice, oil, salt, black pepper and Aleppo pepper. Put the chicken pieces in a baking dish and cover with the marinade. Cover and let marinate in the refrigerator for 12 to 24 hours.

Bake the chicken and marinade together for 30 minutes at 350°F (175°C). Grill the pieces of chicken on the barbeque for about 6 to 8 minutes on each side, until cooked through. Serve with salad and roasted potatoes.

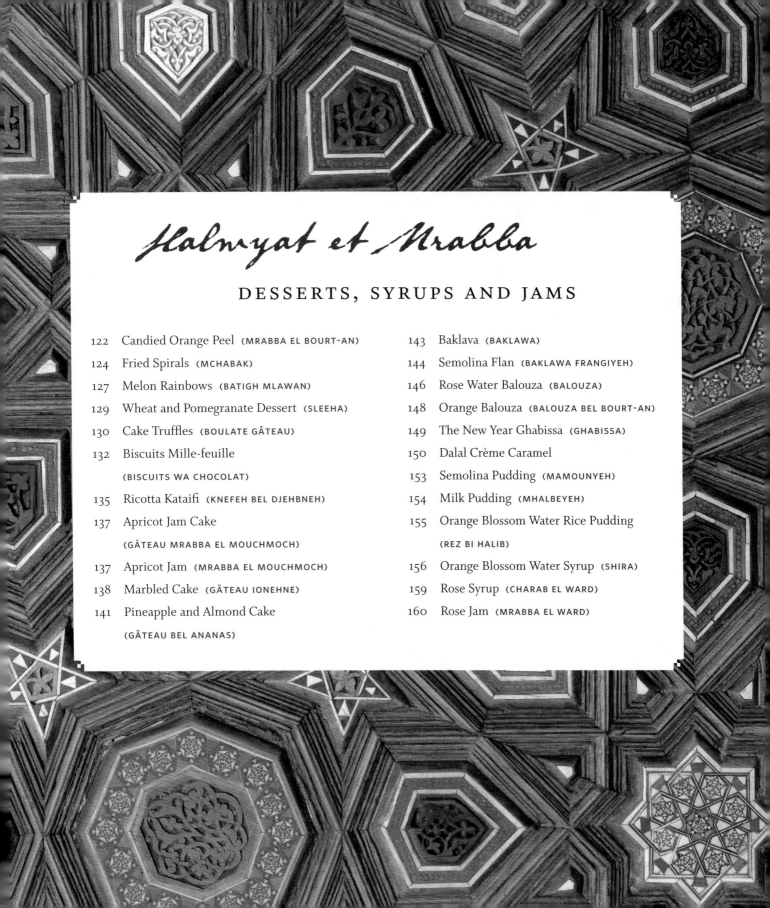

Halwyat et Mrabba

DESSERTS, SYRUPS AND JAMS

Mrabba el Bourt-an

CANDIED ORANGE PEEL

Candied orange peels will keep in the refrigerator for up to a month. One way to enjoy them is with chocolate. Put the candied peels out to dry for 24 hours, to remove any moisture, and then dip them halfway in good-quality melted chocolate. (See photo.) Let them cool on parchment paper before serving.

PREPARATION TIME 15 minutes   **COOKING TIME** 20 TO 30 minutes

10 large oranges with thick skin
1 cup (250 mL) water
6½ cups (1.625 L) granulated
    sugar

Wash and brush the oranges. Cut the root end off and discard. Cut into quarters. Take an orange quarter in one hand. With the other hand, slide the blade of a knife between the pulp and the peel, removing the peel. Cut the peels into sticks ½ inch (1 cm) wide. Put the peels into a large pot, cover with cold water and bring to a boil. Lower the heat and let simmer for 8 to 10 minutes, until tender (prick with a toothpick to test tenderness). Using a colander, drain and rinse several times with cold water to remove the bitterness.

In a pot, add the water and sugar and boil for 5 minutes. Add the orange peels. Cook on low heat for 10 minutes, until candied.

Mchalrat

FRIED SPIRALS

We normally serve this dish for breakfast.

PREPARATION TIME 45 minutes **COOKING TIME** 20 minutes **SERVINGS** 10 to 12

2½ cups (625 mL) fine semolina
    flour
2 tsp (10 mL) baking powder
1 cup (250 mL) yogurt
1¼ cups (310 mL) water
canola oil for frying
1 recipe Orange Blossom Water
    Syrup (page 156)
ground cinnamon

In a bowl, mix the flour with the baking powder using a fork. Add the yogurt and water and stir. Let rest for 30 minutes.

Heat the canola oil in a pot. Put the batter into a large piping bag fitted with a large, star-shaped piping tip. Make spirals 2 to 4 inches (5–10 cm) in diameter on the surface of the hot oil. Fry one side until golden-coloured; turn over and fry the other side the same way.

Pour the Orange Blossom Water Syrup into a large bowl. Remove the spirals from the pot and plunge them into the syrup until they are well soaked. Put the spirals onto a serving dish. Sprinkle with cinnamon. Serve hot.

Batigh Allawan

MELON RAINBOWS

Here is a refreshing and colourful dessert for a sunny day. This recipe makes a large quantity and it is ideal for parties. (For contrasting flavours and colours, pour the lime mixture into the cavity of the cantaloupe, and the strawberry mixture into the cavity of the honeydew melon. For different colours and flavours in one melon, fill half of each melon with one flavour of gelatin. Refrigerate for 30 minutes. Top up each melon with the other flavour of gelatin. Refrigerate for 4 more hours.)

PREPARATION TIME 40 minutes **COOKING TIME** 4 hours **SERVINGS** 20 to 24

1 cantaloupe

1 honeydew melon

3 ounces (85 g) strawberry gelatin

3 ounces (85 g) lime gelatin

1 cup (250 mL) boiling water

1 cup (250 mL) cold water

1 banana, peeled, cut into quarters lengthwise and sliced finely

1 apple, peeled, cut into quarters lengthwise and sliced finely

Peel the cantaloupe and the melon. Cut off a small slice from the end of each to create a stable base. Cut off a ¾-inch (2 cm) slice from the top of each. Remove the tops. Scoop out the seeds with a spoon, making sure not to perforate the flesh. Turn the melons upside down onto paper towels and let drain for 10 to 15 minutes.

In bowls, separately dilute each package of gelatin in ½ cup (125 mL) of boiling water. Mix well until dissolved. Add ½ cup (125 mL) of cold water to each bowl and mix well. Refrigerate for 5 to 10 minutes.

In a bowl, mix the banana and apple. Add half the banana and apple mixture to the strawberry gelatin and half to the lime gelatin; mix to combine. With a spoon, pour the strawberry mixture into the cavity of the cantaloupe, and the lime mixture into the melon. Cover with plastic wrap and refrigerate for 4 hours. Cut into wedges to serve.

WHEAT AND POMEGRANATE DESSERT

Traditionally, *sleeha* is prepared once a year, on December 4, for the feast of Saint Barbara. This celebration is shared with relatives, who teach young family members the importance of helping the less fortunate.

PREPARATION TIME 12 hours **COOKING TIME** 1 to 1½ hours **SERVINGS** 10 to 12

1¾ pounds (875 g) whole wheat kernels

1¼ cups (310 mL) granulated sugar

3 Tbsp (45 mL) fennel seeds, toasted and ground

1 tsp (5 mL) ground cinnamon

1 cup (250 mL) walnuts

1 cup (250 mL) raisins

1½ to 2 cups (375–500 mL) pomegranate seeds

Soak the whole wheat kernels in cold water for 12 hours. Strain. In a pot, add the strained kernels and cover with water. Bring to a boil. Reduce the heat to low and cook for 1 to 1½ hours, until completely cooked. Remove from the heat. Add the sugar, fennel seeds and cinnamon and mix well. Add the walnuts and raisins and mix well. Add the pomegranate seeds and mix well. Serve warm.

Boulate Gâteau

CAKE TRUFFLES

In Aleppo, we normally get this dessert at the bakery. Once we came to Quebec, I had to find the exact amounts of ingredients through trial and error to reproduce the refined taste of this confectionary.

PREPARATION TIME 15 minutes   **COOKING TIME** 5 minutes   **YIELD** 55 to 60 truffles

1 recipe Marbled Cake (page 138)

1½ cups (375 mL) Candied Orange Peel (page 122), chopped roughly

1 tsp (5 mL) ground cloves

1 cup (250 mL) walnuts, chopped roughly

7 ounces (200 g) dark chocolate, melted

1½ pounds (750 g) dark chocolate, melted, for coating

In a bowl, break up the Marbled Cake. Add the Candied Orange Peel, cloves, walnuts and the 7 ounces (200 g) of melted dark chocolate. Mix well. With the dough, make balls the size of golf balls. Dip each truffle into the 1½ pounds (750 g) of melted dark chocolate. Place on a parchment paper–lined cookie sheet to cool. Serve in decorative candy cups.

Biscuits ma Chocolat

BISCUITS MILLE-FEUILLE

When I was only five years old, I made this dessert with my mother. I continue the tradition of making this dessert with my children.

PREPARATION TIME 4 to 6 hours **SERVINGS** 10 to 12

13 ounces (400 g) 72% dark
   chocolate
1 cup (250 mL) 35% cream
60 tea biscuits (purchased)
¾ cup (185 mL) strong espresso
   coffee or orange juice
raspberries, for garnish

Line an 8- × 8-inch (20 × 20 cm) pan with plastic wrap, draping the wrap over the sides.

In a pot, melt the chocolate on medium heat with the cream. Set aside half of the melted chocolate mixture and refrigerate.

Dip 10 biscuits in the coffee (making sure the whole biscuit gets dipped) and arrange in a layer on the bottom of the pan. Cover with a thin layer of chocolate. Repeat the biscuit and chocolate layers, making five layers and finishing with a biscuit layer. Bring the plastic wrap up over the biscuit to cover the *mille-feuille* (use more plastic wrap if needed). Refrigerate for 4 to 6 hours.

Re-melt the remaining chocolate and cream mixture on low heat. Remove the plastic wrap and turn the *mille-feuille* upside down onto a serving plate. Pour the melted chocolate overtop and decorate with raspberries. Let the chocolate set and become cold before serving.

Knefeh bel Djehbneh

RICOTTA KATAIFI

Shredded phyllo pastry, called *kataifi*, is available in Middle Eastern grocery stores.

PREPARATION TIME 12 to 24 hours   **COOKING TIME** 1 hour   **SERVINGS** 10 to 12

1 pound (500 g) ricotta cheese

2 Tbsp (30 mL) granulated sugar

1 pound (500 g) kataifi
(shredded phyllo pastry;
pictured on page 136)

10 ounces (300 g) butter, melted

1 cup (250 mL) Orange Blossom
Water Syrup (page 156)

Generously butter a 12- × 8-inch (30 × 20 cm) baking dish. In a bowl, mix the ricotta and sugar. Set aside.

In another bowl, separate the kataifi threads with your fingers (see page 136). Pour the melted butter overtop and gently stir to coat the kataifi threads evenly. Spread out half of the kataifi mixture over the bottom of the baking dish. Press into place. Spread the ricotta evenly overtop. Cover evenly with the remaining kataifi mixture. Press firmly into place. Cover with plastic wrap directly on the surface of the kataifi. (You can add weight, such as a plate filled with water, on top of the plastic to increase the pressure on the kataifi.) Let rest in the refrigerator for 12 to 24 hours.

Preheat the oven to 350°F (175°C). In the pan, cut the kataifi into 2-inch (5 cm) squares. Bake for about 1 hour, until golden-coloured. Remove from the oven and glaze immediately with the Orange Blossom Water Syrup.

KATAIFI (SHREDDED PHYLLO PASTRY) IS USED IN RICOTTA KATAIFI (PAGE 135)

Gâteau Mrabba el Mouchmoch

APRICOT JAM CAKE

PREPARATION TIME 15 minutes   **COOKING TIME** 45 minutes   **SERVINGS** 10 to 12

2 eggs

2 cups (500 mL) all-purpose
   flour

1 cup (250 mL) granulated sugar

1 tsp (5 mL) baking soda

½ cup (125 mL) butter, at room
   temperature

1 tsp (5 mL) vanilla extract

zest of 1 lemon

1½ cups (375 mL) Apricot Jam
   (below)

Preheat the oven to 350°F (175°C). Butter a 10-inch (25 cm) round baking dish and set aside. In a large bowl, using a fork, mix the eggs, flour, sugar, baking soda, butter, vanilla and zest. Separate the dough into two balls. Spread one ball over the bottom of the baking dish. Spread the jam evenly overtop. Cover with the other half of the dough. Bake for 45 minutes. Cool.

Mrabba el Mouchmoch

APRICOT JAM

PREPARATION TIME 24 hours   **COOKING TIME** 3½ to 6½ hours   **YIELD** 8 to 10 jars

3⅓ pounds (1.6 kg) fresh
   apricots

2 pounds (1 kg) granulated sugar

Cut the apricots in half and remove the pits. Arrange the fruit on the bottom of a large pot, cut-side up. Cover with the sugar and let sit for 12 hours. Cook the apricots on low heat until the sugar dissolves. Remove the apricots and strain. Reduce the syrup for 3 to 4 hours on low heat. Add the apricots and cook for 30 minutes more. Turn off the heat and let cool overnight. (If the syrup is too clear, remove the apricots and reduce the syrup for 1 to 2 hours more.) Pour into jars.

Gâteau Jonehne

MARBLED CAKE

When our children were small, we always brought this cake with us on trips. Very easy to make and very tasty, this dessert is a must for my family. Keep a few pieces to make Cake Truffles (page 130). If you don't want to use butter in this cake, you could use 1 cup (250 mL) of canola oil. For a different taste, replace the walnuts with the same amount of raisins.

PREPARATION TIME 15 minutes **COOKING TIME** 1 hour **SERVINGS** 10 to 12

½ cup (125 mL) butter, at room temperature

2 cups (500 mL) granulated sugar

6 eggs

1 tsp (5 mL) pure vanilla extract

½ cup (125 mL) orange juice

2 Tbsp (30 mL) arak or another alcohol (optional)

3 cups (750 mL) all-purpose flour, sifted

2 tsp (10 mL) baking powder

½ cup (125 mL) milk

6 Tbsp (90 mL) cocoa powder

¾ cup (185 mL) walnuts, chopped roughly

icing sugar, for dusting

Preheat the oven to 350°F (175°C). Butter and flour a Bundt pan. Set aside.

In a large bowl, using an electric mixer, beat the butter and sugar. Add the eggs and vanilla. Mix well. Gradually, in turn, add ¼ cup (60 mL) of the orange juice, and the arak, flour, baking powder and milk. Pour half of this batter into the pan. To the remaining batter in the bowl, add the cocoa powder, the remaining ¼ cup (60 mL) of orange juice and the walnuts. Mix well. Pour the cocoa batter overtop the orange juice batter in the pan.

With a skewer or knife, draw light zigzags into the batter to make the marbling. Bake for 1 hour. Remove the cake from the oven. Let cool for 10 minutes before turning out of the pan. Dust with icing sugar.

Gâteau bel Ananas

PINEAPPLE AND ALMOND CAKE

This cake is my husband's favourite. He tasted it for the first time 30 years ago, when my mother made it, and I continue to make it each year for his birthday. If you like, you can garnish the centre of the pineapple slices with raspberries.

PREPARATION TIME 30 minutes **COOKING TIME** 1½ hours **SERVINGS** 10 to 12

PASTRY CREAM
4 eggs

4 Tbsp (60 mL) granulated sugar

2 Tbsp (30 mL) all-purpose flour

zest of 1 lemon

1 tsp (5 mL) pure vanilla extract

4 cups (1 L) milk

CAKE
3 cups (750 mL) all-purpose flour

2 tsp (10 mL) baking powder

6 eggs

1 cup (250 mL) canola oil

2 cups (500 mL) granulated sugar

½ cup (125 mL) orange juice

½ cup (125 mL) milk

GARNISH
two 14-ounce (398 mL) cans sliced pineapple, in its juice

½ cup (125 mL) blanched almonds, chopped finely

PASTRY CREAM | In a large pot, mix the eggs, sugar, flour, zest and vanilla. Slowly pour in the milk and whisk. Cook on medium heat, while stirring, until thickened. Remove from heat. Allow to cook for 15 minutes longer by leaving on the counter. Mix well. Lay plastic wrap directly on the surface of cream. Cool in the refrigerator. (The pastry cream can be made 12 to 24 hours in advance.)

CAKE | Preheat the oven to 350°F (175°C). Butter and flour a 12-inch (30 cm) round pan. Set aside. Sift the flour and baking powder. Set aside. In a bowl, beat the eggs, canola oil and sugar with an electric mixer for 4 to 5 minutes. Alternate adding the dry ingredients and the orange juice and milk, a bit at a time, mixing after each addition of wet and dry. Pour the mixture into the pan. Bake for 1 hour. Remove from the oven and let cool for 10 minutes before turning out of the pan.

ASSEMBLY | Holding a knife parallel to the counter, cut the cake in half to create two layers. Set the layers side by side, cut-sides up. **(CONTINUED ON NEXT PAGE)**

PINEAPPLE AND ALMOND CAKE (CONTINUED FROM PAGE 141)

Sprinkle each layer with the pineapple juice from the cans. Taking pineapple slices from 1 can, chop them finely. Set aside. Spread a quarter of the pastry cream on the lower tier of the cake. Spread the chopped pineapple overtop. Sprinkle with ¼ cup (60 mL) of the almonds. Cover with the top tier of the cake. Ice the top and sides of the cake with the remaining pastry cream. Sprinkle with the remaining almonds. Garnish with the reserved pineapple slices.

BAKLAVA

PREPARATION TIME 10 minutes   **COOKING TIME** 45 to 60 minutes   **SERVINGS** 10 to 12

1¼ cups (310 mL) walnuts, chopped finely

3 Tbsp (45 mL) granulated sugar

2 Tbsp (30 mL) orange blossom water

1 pound (500 g) phyllo pastry

1 cup (250 mL) butter, melted

Orange Blossom Water Syrup (page 156), for sprinkling

Generously butter a 12- × 9-inch (30 × 23 cm) baking dish. In a bowl, mix the walnuts, sugar and orange blossom water. Set aside.

Unroll the phyllo and cut the sheets in half down the centre, widthwise. Lay out half of the phyllo pastry sheets in the baking dish and brush with half of the melted butter. Spread out the walnut mixture. Cover with the rest of the phyllo pastry and brush with the rest of the melted butter. In the pan, cut the baklava into 2-inch (5 cm) squares. Bake for 45 to 60 minutes. Sprinkle with Orange Blossom Water Syrup. Serve warm.

Batlama Frangiyeh

SEMOLINA FLAN

Every time my mother makes this dessert, it flies out the window like hotcakes.
She doesn't even have time to let it cool before a few small slices disappear.

PREPARATION TIME 24 hours   **COOKING TIME** 45 to 60 minutes   **SERVINGS** 10 to 15

4 eggs
1 tsp (5 mL) vanilla extract
8 cups (2 L) milk
1½ cups (375 mL) fine semolina
icing sugar
ground cinnamon

Generously butter a 9- × 12-inch (23 × 30 cm) baking dish. In a bowl, beat the eggs and vanilla extract with a fork. Set aside.

In a heavy-bottomed pot, heat the milk on medium heat; do not boil. While stirring constantly, sprinkle in the semolina. Cook, stirring often, until the batter thickens. While stirring, add the egg and vanilla mixture. Pour into the dish and let cool for about an hour, to room temperature. Cover with plastic wrap and refrigerate until the next day, to allow the mixture to set.

Preheat the oven to 350°F (175°C). In the pan, cut the flan into ¾-inch (2 cm) squares. Bake for 45 to 60 minutes, until golden-coloured. Remove from the oven and let sit for 30 minutes, to room temperature. Using a sieve, generously sprinkle with the icing sugar and cinnamon. Serve warm.

Balouza

ROSE WATER BALOUZA

We take pleasure making classic, refreshing, fragrant desserts like this one. For balouza with orange blossom water, replace the rose water with orange blossom water. This will give the drink a pale white rather than a pink colour (also omit the pink food colouring and edible rose petals). See photo for Rose Water Balouza (bottom right), balouza with orange blossom water (top) and Orange Balouza (bottom left).

PREPARATION TIME 15 minutes **COOKING TIME** 15 minutes **SERVINGS** 12

7 cups (1.75 L) water

1 cup (250 mL) cornstarch

¾ cup (185 mL) cold water

2 cups (500 mL) granulated sugar

2 Tbsp (30 mL) rose water

a few drops of pink food colouring

1 cup (250 mL) Aleppo pistachios, blanched

edible rose petals, for garnish

In a large, heavy-bottomed pot, heat the 7 cups (1.75 L) of water without bringing to a boil.

In a bowl, dilute the cornstarch with the ¾ cup (185 mL) cold water. Pour into the hot water and cook, stirring constantly, until thickened, about 3 minutes. Add the sugar and stir to dissolve. Continue cooking until thickened again. Remove from the heat. Add the rose water, food colouring and pistachios. Mix well. Pour into glasses or ramekins and let cool to room temperature. Cover and refrigerate for at least 2 hours. Decorate with rose petals.

Balouza bel Bourt-an

ORANGE BALOUZA

Pictured on page 147.

PREPARATION TIME 15 minutes **COOKING TIME** 15 minutes **SERVINGS** 12

5¼ cups (1.85 L) water

one 12-ounce (355 mL) can frozen concentrated orange juice

1 cup (250 mL) cornstarch

¾ cup (185 mL) cold water

3 cups (750 mL) granulated sugar

1 cup (250 mL) blanched almonds, halved

1 cup (250 mL) orange peel slivers

In a large, heavy-bottomed pot, heat the 5¼ cups (1.85 L) water and concentrated orange juice without bringing to a boil.

In a bowl, dilute the cornstarch with the ¾ cup (185 mL) cold water. Pour into the hot water and juice mixture and bring to a boil. Let boil for 3 to 5 minutes, stirring constantly, until thickened. Add the sugar and cook for 2 to 3 minutes. Stir. Remove from heat and add the almonds and the orange peel slivers. Pour into glasses or ramekins and let cool to room temperature. Cover and refrigerate for at least 2 hours.

ghabissa

THE NEW YEAR GHABISSA

For this dish, tradition dictates that the serving plate be scented with incense before this pudding-like dish is put onto it, to impart the delicate perfume.

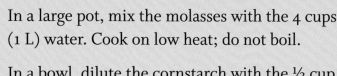

PREPARATION TIME 15 minutes   **COOKING TIME** 15 to 20 minutes   **SERVINGS** 12 to 14

2 cups (500 mL) raisin molasses

4 cups (1 L) water

¾ cup (185 mL) cornstarch

½ cup (125 mL) water

½ cup (125 mL) granulated sugar

1½ tsp (7 mL) ground ginger

1 cup (250 mL) walnuts, cut in half and toasted

In a large pot, mix the molasses with the 4 cups (1 L) water. Cook on low heat; do not boil.

In a bowl, dilute the cornstarch with the ½ cup (125 mL) water. Add the cornstarch mixture to the molasses. Bring to a boil on medium heat and cook, stirring constantly, for 4 to 5 minutes, until thickened. Add the sugar and ginger. Continue to cook, stirring constantly, for 1 to 2 minutes. Pour into a 12-inch (30 cm) plate or into bowls. Garnish with the walnuts and refrigerate for 1 hour.

DALAL CRÈME CARAMEL

PREPARATION TIME 15 minutes   **COOKING TIME** 1 hour   **SERVINGS** 10 to 12

6 cups (1.5 L) milk

1¼ cups (310 mL) granulated
sugar

1 cup (250 mL) granulated sugar

½ tsp (2 mL) fresh lemon juice

12 eggs

½ tsp (2 mL) lemon zest

2 tsp (10 mL) pure vanilla extract

In a pot, cook the milk and 1¼ cups (310 mL) granulated sugar on medium heat until the sugar dissolves. Remove from the heat and let cool to room temperature. Preheat the oven to 400°F (200°C).

To another pot, add the 1 cup (250 mL) granulated sugar and the lemon juice. On high heat, cook until caramel-coloured. Pour into a Bundt pan, coating the contours well. Place the Bundt pan into a large, high-sided baking sheet.

In a bowl, beat the eggs with the lemon zest and the vanilla. Add to the milk and sugar mixture. Mix well and pour into the Bundt pan.

To make a *bain-marie* (water bath), pour hot water into the baking sheet halfway up the Bundt pan. Put into the oven and bake for 1 hour. Remove from the oven. Remove the Bundt pan from the *bain-marie* and let cool to room temperature. Refrigerate for 12 hours. To turn out the crème caramel from the Bundt pan, slide a knife around the edges of the pan. Gently tip out onto a large serving dish.

Mamounyeh

SEMOLINA PUDDING

PREPARATION TIME 5 minutes **COOKING TIME** 15 to 30 minutes **SERVINGS** 4

4 cups (1 L) water

2 cups (500 mL) granulated
sugar

4 Tbsp (60 mL) butter

1 cup (250 mL) fine semolina

ground cinnamon, for garnish

4 Tbsp (60 mL) ricotta, for
garnish

pistachios, crushed, for garnish

In a large pot, boil the water and sugar for 3 to 4 minutes.

In another large pot, on medium heat, melt the butter. Add the semolina and cook, while stirring, until golden-coloured. Add the boiling syrup and mix. Turn off the heat, cover and let rest for 5 minutes. Serve in a bowl, sprinkled with cinnamon and garnished with a bit of ricotta and crushed pistachios. Accompany this dish with pita and braided cheese. (See page 3 for a note on making braided cheese.)

Mhalbeyeh

MILK PUDDING

For an interesting visual effect, fill half of a clear, individual dessert bowl with this milk pudding. Add the same amount of brightly coloured gelatin (for example, strawberry) overtop.

PREPARATION TIME 10 to 15 minutes **COOKING TIME** 10 minutes **SERVINGS** 12

1¼ cups (310 mL) cornstarch
8 cups (2 L) milk
1 cup (250 mL) granulated sugar
2 Tbsp (30 mL) orange blossom
    water
ground cinnamon

Dilute the cornstarch in 1 cup (250 mL) of the milk. Set aside. In a pot, heat the remaining milk on medium heat, without bringing to a boil. Add the cornstarch and milk mixture and stir until thickened. Stir in the sugar and cook for 2 to 3 minutes. Remove from the heat, add the orange blossom water and mix well. Pour into individual bowls. Let rest for a few minutes, cover and refrigerate. Sprinkle with cinnamon, to taste, before serving.

Rez bi Halib

ORANGE BLOSSOM WATER RICE PUDDING

My husband and children like eating this dish with cheese for lunch.

PREPARATION TIME 10 minutes **COOKING TIME** 1 hour **SERVINGS** 10 to 12

8 cups (2 L) milk

1¼ cups (310 mL) medium-grain rice, well rinsed

1 cup (250 mL) granulated sugar

2 Tbsp (30 mL) orange blossom water

ground cinnamon

In a heavy-bottomed pot, heat the milk on medium heat without bringing to a boil. Add the rice and sugar and mix well. Reduce the heat to low. Let simmer, stirring frequently, for 40 to 60 minutes until thickened. Remove from the heat. Add the orange blossom water and stir gently. Pour into individual bowls. Let cool for 30 minutes, cover and refrigerate. Sprinkle with ground cinnamon to taste and serve.

ORANGE BLOSSOM WATER SYRUP

This syrup is used to saturate many Middle Eastern pastries. It is impossible to speak of Aleppian cuisine without orange blossom water, which possesses a characteristic perfumed flavour. Since this syrup keeps for several months, I prepare it in large quantities.

PREPARATION TIME 5 minutes **COOKING TIME** 10 minutes **YIELD** 2 cups (500 mL)

2 cups (500 mL) granulated
   sugar
1 cup (250 mL) water
1 Tbsp (15 mL) orange blossom
   water

In a large pot on high heat, add the sugar and water and boil for 8 to 10 minutes. Remove from the heat and add the orange blossom water. Cool.

Charab el Ward

ROSE SYRUP

To make a refreshing drink, greatly appreciated in the summer, pour ¼ cup (60 mL) of this syrup and ¾ cup (185 mL) of water into a large glass. Stir, add crushed ice and garnish with fresh mint.

PREPARATION TIME 5 minutes   **COOKING TIME** 5 to 10 minutes   **YIELD** 4 to 5 cups (1–1.2 L)

4 cups (1 L) water
10 cups (2.5 L) granulated sugar
1 Tbsp (15 mL) fresh lemon juice
one 10½-ounce (300 mL) bottle
    of rose water
a few drops of red food colouring

In a large, heavy-bottomed pot, bring the water, sugar and lemon juice to a boil for 5 minutes. Add the rose water and a few drops of food colouring until pink-coloured. Let boil for 1 minute.

Mrabba el Ward

ROSE JAM

The Hansa rose is an ancient variety of rose with very fragrant, purplish double flowers. The Hansa rosebush is a rustic one that is found in many gardens in Aleppo.

PREPARATION TIME 3 to 4 hours   **YIELD** 10 to 12 jars

2 pounds (1 kg) whole Hansa roses (with bases)
2 cups (500 mL) fresh lemon juice
5 cups (1.25 L) water
¼ tsp (1 mL) citric acid
5½ pounds (2.5 kg) granulated sugar

Pull the petals from the roses and put small quantities at a time in a colander. Without rinsing the petals, mix them with your fingers to remove the dirt.

Put the petals in a large bowl. Add the lemon juice and knead for a few minutes. Press between your palms to extract as much liquid as possible. Reserve the liquid.

Put the rose petals into a pressure cooker. Add the water and citric acid. Close the cooker tightly and turn the heat to high. When the cooker begins to whistle, lower the heat and let simmer for 30 minutes. Run cold water over the cooker to bring the pressure down. Open the cooker and turn the heat back to high for 15 to 20 minutes to eliminate excess water. Add the sugar and boil for 10 minutes. Remove from the heat. Add the reserved rose liquid and mix well.

Fill a large container with water and ice. Put the cooker into it. Stir the jam until it cools completely. Leave the jam in the cooker until the next day. Pour into jars.

INDEX